Reloading
A Practical
Hobby

Richard M. Beloin MD

authorHOUSE®

AuthorHouse™
1663 Liberty Drive
Bloomington, IN 47403
www.authorhouse.com
Phone: 1 (800) 839-8640

Published by AuthorHouse 10/19/2017

ISBN: 978-1-5462-0989-8 (sc)
ISBN: 978-1-5462-0987-4 (hc)
ISBN: 978-1-5462-0988-1 (e)

Library of Congress Control Number: 2017914853

Print information available on the last page.

Dedication

This book is dedicated to my wife Claudette of nearly 50years. For encouraging me to write and helping me with printing, organization, proof reading and editing.

Table of Contents

CHAPTER-1

INTRODUCTION & ACKNOWLEDGMENT

INTRODUCTION

The most difficult part in writing a book is finding the right words to get started. Not only do you need to grasp the readers attention, you must also concisely describe the contents of the book.

Right from the start, I am proud to state that I am a Dillon man—I have used a Square Deal B and I am now using a XL 650 as well as some other accessories. I also use accessories from RCBS, Hornady, Lyman and Lee. From Lee I use the C-arm adjuvant reloading press and the 30-30 factory crimp. RCBS provides the rifle dies. For rifle bullets and a manual trimmer, I use Hornady. Lyman products include their turret press/powder measure, handheld chamfering/deburring tool, and their E–Zee pistol/rifle case length gage. My balance beam scale is from Redding.

The proposal that reloading can be a practical hobby has the prerequisite that you belong to a shooting sport or similar endeavor. Belonging to a shooting sport needs the production of large volumes of quality ammo. Without the need to practice and compete you become a sporadic or occasional reloader of hunting and plinking/target ammo. In comparison, if you compete in Cowboy Action Shooting or USPSA, you will need large amounts of ammo for practice and competition. When I was training for these two sports, it was common to send at least a thousand rounds down range per week and then bring several hundred rounds for competition. The drive to support my habit was the stimulus to become a regular and practical reloader.

Reloading is a continuous learning process. We often forget knowledge and methods when we don't reload regularly. It all depends whether you reload so you can shoot more freely or whether you shoot so you can get back to reloading. Reloading should be a pleasure and not an activity to "get it out of the way". I reload because I enjoy it and I can shoot more freely. Reloading is the most economical way to enjoy the shooting sports.

As a practical method, I will describe my reloading routine during a loading session for bulk pistol ammo and another session when loading rifle hunting ammo. These sessions involve the use of modern "tools of the trade". It follows that these tools cover the major subject matter of this book. The hobby reloader not only enjoys the process, he or she wants to work with great tools—as covered in Chapters 2–6. Other chapters will cover: primers, new powders, new bullet types, special topics and much more.

To clarify a point, this book is not about F Class competition that includes benchrest and long range rifle shooting. The entire basis of handloading for this class requires more equipment precision and extra techniques to yield the best rifle accuracy possible. This entire subject and equipment is not part of this book. This book is about practical reloading–the production of volume/quality pistol ammo and limited rifle hunting ammo.

ACKNOWLEDGMENT

The contents of this book cover more than my experiences during forty years of reloading. I am an organizer and have researched the subject for months over many long hours. I reviewed reloading manuals, Dillon forums, Brian Enos forums, articles from the experts and multiple shooting/reloading forums to include: the firearms forum, the firing line forum, reloaders nest forum, handloader bench forum and many others. Included in the research was a reproduction of the proper products descriptions in manufacturers catalogs and retailers web sites. My best source of information was the Dillon web site to include the following forums: Dillon reloading equipment–Square Deal B

–XL 650
–other Dillon equipment
Dillon Reloading–Rifle calibers
–Handgun calibers

The real benefit of these Dillon forums is the fact that the expert discussant was an actual Customer Service representative. I have referred to many retail sites for these tools and reloading components. I have used and acknowledged Dillon, Brownells, Midway, Cabelas, Amazon, ebay and gunbroker.

My most important acknowledgment is the heavily footnoted and referenced portion of this book. I strongly believe that the sites, forums and authors be appropriately recognized. I have over 20 pages of references and I am proud that I am the organizer of these sources.

With this preface, I present this publication for your pleasure.

DILLON XL 650 PRESS

Introduction

1. Blue Press specifications/prices

   A–Press and casefeeder

   B–Optional items

2. Powder Check

   A–Dillon

   B–RCBS lockout die

   C–Relative significance of a double charge

3. Other Dillon XL 650 options

   A–Tool holder

   B–Strong mount

   C–Roller handle

   D–Bullet tray

   E–Low powder sensor

   F–Dust cover

   G–Spare parts kit/spring kit

4. Lubrication

   A–Materials

   B–Lubrication points

5. Casefeeder

   A–Plate clutch

   B–Funnel adapter

   C–Failure to feed

   D–Jamming plate

   E–Cases not entering shellplate

   F–Upside down cases

6. Interruption of case and primer feed

   A–Priming system

   B–Casefeed system

7. Humidity

8. Reloaders shoulder

Introduction

WHAT IS A DILLON XL 650? It is a high-speed progressive reloading machine designed to load the common rifle and handgun cartridges. This machine is capable of producing up to 800 rounds per hour with the use of the XL

650 casefeeder. Dillon offers a 30 day free trial and if you purchase one, it comes with a "lifetime no BS warranty".

It is a common opinion in the shooting forums that this machine is a mechanical masterpiece and a true turnkey system. It has a short learning curve, free of wasted time from repeated tweaking and simply easy to keep running.[4k]

I reload for pleasure and so I want a press that is a joy to use. Quite simply, this press "loads and loads and loads" with the most incredible smoothness and reliability.

1. Blue Press specifications/prices

A–Press and casefeeder.

I purchase all my Dillon products thru the Blue Press catalog via on line or phone orders. The press and casefeeder sells for $785 and includes the following:[1a]

- 5 station auto indexing
- 500–800 rounds per hour
- one caliber conversion
- one 5 station toolhead
- automatic powder measure
- automatic primer system

B–Optional features include:[1a]

- roller handle($46)
- powder check system($69)

- 4 large pickup tubes($24)
- 4 small pickup tubes($24)
- spare parts kit($26)
- each additional conversion kits($78)
- extra toolhead($28)
- extra powder dies($11)
- three-die carbide dies set($66)
- flip tray($21)
- RF–100 automatic primer filler for "S and L" primers($325)

2. Powder Check

A–Dillon.

This powder check is the number one item on my list of optional items that belong in the necessity category. If you want to be safe, DON'T BE CHEAP, because this is the most important accessory in the press. You can rely on this die to warn you of a "double charge" or of a "no charge". Both of these events can ruin more than your day.

In addition it will alert you to a problem that is robbing powder in small increments which is so important if you are loading 3+- grains of fast powders for cowboy shooting. This powder check will also warn you of "stepped up cases"–a situation where a case has a high base and corresponding smaller case volume. This lower case volume is crucial if you are loading near max–a dangerous high pressure may result.[11a]

B–RCBS

The RCBS lock-out die will stop the 650 press if there is too much or not enough powder. It's major use is in double charges or absent charges(squib load). The drawback is that it works only with straight wall cases.[24/28]

Other issues is that it is not a powder check that will check for small variances in powder as in stepped up cases or in powder robbing situations. It is not very useful with powder loads less than 3+- grains since it acts as an empty case.[23a]

C–Relative significance of a double charge

A double charge of Clays when you are loading 3 grains in a 38 case would give you a charge of 6 grains of Clays. I am certain that my NRV can handle this double charge. I regularly shoot 6 grains of Titegroup in my old style 44 mag Vaquero–could it handle 12 gr.? This may not be the case if using old guns or generic substitutes with poor quality steel. Either way, a double charge is just not acceptable and is an embarrassing situation for the shooter during a competition since all the participants know what happened. Here is a true experience worth mentioning.

For years I reloaded using the auto indexing Square Deal B and I upgraded to a Dillon RL 550 which does not have auto indexing or a slot for a powder check. With this background I went to a cowboy shoot and while on the firing line I had a double charge. Remember that I had gone from an auto indexing press to a manually indexing RL 550 and I admit that I had trouble remembering to index the shellplate. Needless to say I was embarrassed to the max so I called Dillon to trade my RL 550 for an XL 650. The customer agent was hesitant to make the trade since I was over my 30 day trial period. So I told the agent about my experience at the cowboy shoot but added that the range officer asked me, in plain ear shot of all to hear, which press I was using and I answered very loudly "Dillon RL 550". There was no need to say anymore–I had an XL 650 four days later at no charge and a powder check at my cost.

There are situations as serious as a double charge that are worth mentioning that can lead to disastrous results. A few are as follows:[6a]

- Unrecognized squib load
- Using the wrong powder
- Dumping powder in the wrong powder container
- Loading a round above max charge
- Forcing a pistol slide forward with a stuck case in the chamber

3. Other Dillon XL 650 options.[2b]

A–Toolholder($20–30) Holds the tools you need to service your reloader with or without wrench set.

B–Strong mount($50) A rise mount of 6 inches. Allows you to use any location on the bench instead of only the edge of the bench. It also enables the attachment of other accessories.

C–Roller handle($46) This item reduces operator fatigue, makes primer seating easy and helps in controlling the priming arm from accidental detonations(more later).

D–Bullet tray($43) A shallow aluminum tray located for economy of motion and attached to the strong mount.

E–Low powder sensor($42) It provides an audible reminder when it is time to refill the powder reservoir.

F–Dust cover($40) Not only a neat cover but it locks as well.

G–Spare parts kit($27) There are 46 parts in the XL 650 kit. Great value. Just call Dillon for any individual part and find an easy $5 charge plus shipping if the part is not on warranty. Over the years I have used these parts regularly and try to bunch my replacement orders as much as possible.[2b]

Springs are the items needed the most. They break or weaken and need to be replaced. I keep extras of the most frequently changed springs. These are as follows: (reference is made to the 6.1 version of the manual)

- casefeed arm return spring 13936 page 52
- case insert slide spring 13937 page 54(most common replaced)
- ring indexer return spring 13791 page 54
- primer locator tab spring 13624 page 55
- primer indexing arm spring 13965 page 55

There are some parts that I keep as spare since they are the ones that tend to get lost by rolling or flying away. There are three. The index ball 13891 page 54, the primer disc ball 13932 page 55, and the powder measure bell crank cube 13871 page 56. There is also one item that tends to fail and that is the micro-switch on the casefeed assembly 13779 page 57. When this switch fails, you are back to manually loading cases.

Over the years and over 300,000 rounds, other parts have failed and needed replacement. Fortunately the "no BS warranty" generally covers these parts. It is impossible to keep an inventory for all possible situations. Other than these specific parts held as backup, you need to rely on Dillon's great customer service and the US mail service.

4. Lubrication.

A–Materials.

Plastic parts erode, dissolve and split when exposed to petroleum based solvents and lubricants. Always use synthetic heavy bearing grease on the plastic parts. I use Mobil One synthetic bearing grease and a tub will cost you $9. There are many other brands and one example is the Mil-Comm TW25B synthetic grease. It is available in sizes from a 0.5 ounce syringe to an 8 ounce tub. The economical grease gun tubes are available in synthetic grease for $10 per tube. Any lubricant not free of petroleum products is not made for your press–go synthetic because it is thick and sticks to all plastic and metal parts. The only exception is the priming shaft which should be oiled with 30 weight motor oil.[1d]

B–Lubrication points.

The best video of all the points to grease is available on youtube.com. Look for "Lubrication of the Dillon precision XL 650". Generally apply the grease with a Q-tip to the following points:[25a] (easier to follow with video)

- all pivot pins–Zerk fittings with grease gun or grease holes with syringe.
- main shaft pivot pin–loosen the set screw at the bottom of the priming shaft and push the pin out ½ inch either direction

- interior of ring indexer, cam surface of ring indexer and indexer block
- primer slide cam
- lift station 1 indicator and lube the underside and the side railings that the case insert slide rides on
- underside of shellplate bolt where it contacts with the shellplate if not using the bearing kit(mentioned in upgrades)
- rails of powder measure body where powder measure rides on
- roller of connector body collar of powder measure
- primer disc pin of priming system[25a]

5. Casefeeder.

The powered casefeeder is the equipment that makes the XL 650 the quality tool that it is. Cases are fed into station one with ease and very few operational problems. Listed here are some of the minor issues that can easily be corrected.

A–Casefeeder plate/clutch. The clutch should be able to handle a standard load of 350 count 38 cases or 400 count 9mm cases WITHOUT SLIPPING. If it is slipping, tighten the two screws on the casefeeder plate. If a case locks up the rotation of the plate, the clutch should slip or it can damage the motor. Fine tuning is needed to avoid slipping during normal operation yet allow slipping when a blockage occurs.[1s]

B–Casefeeder funnel adapter. There is a white T shaped

adapter that fits in the old style rectangular funnel. The new style round funnels do not need it. It is used with short cases such as 9mm that tend to jam up and plug the funnel.[4c]

C–Failure to feed. There are usually four causes.[4d/4e] To understand this section please refer to the manual 6.1version "casefeed body assembly" on page 52 to visualize the terms—casefeed adapter, arm, arm bushing, arm stop pin, body bushing, arm return spring and black case slide cam.

The first—once a case falls in the long tube, if it does not feed properly it is because of a problem with the casefeeder adapter(the 3 inch plastic adapter at end of tube) or the casefeeder arm bushing(the ½ inch long colored plastic insert in the arm). The usual solution is to line up the two since the connection tends to bend with use.[4d]

The second cause is a loose black case slide cam that is not pushing the arm bushing enough. Tightening the screw and repositioning the slide will resolve this issue.[4d]

The third cause is that the casefeed arm is not going back enough. This is usually because the arm spring is broken or weakened and needs to be replaced. There is also a casefeed arm stop pin that may have loosened and needs to be tightened back in its place.[4d]

The fourth cause is the body bushing(the metal piece below the arm bushing). It may be screwed in too tight and is rubbing on the arm or the plastic bushing. Simply loosening the body bushing will solve the problem.[4e]

D–Jamming plate. Cases are getting jammed between the plate and frame before they fall in the funnel. There are four solutions:[4f]

- Do not over fill the hopper(max 350 38 specials)
- Use the slow speed on the casefeeder motor
- Slide the frame metal tab under the plate out–to shorten the gap to the funnel
- Clean the rotating plate and fingers. These get sticky and it is enough to delay the case from falling in the funnel[4f]

E–Cases not entering shellplate

It is generally accepted that when cases fail to enter the shellplate, minor adjustments are needed as follows:[1e]

- Slow down your loading speed
- A loose shellplate causes a speed bump as the case slides from the guide to the plate
- Movement of the shell guide during the feed process may be a cause. This is resolved by applying a dab of grease on the bottom of the shell guide. The grease dampens the guide and holds it in place during feeding
- Keep the case slide cam tight. The screw that holds it to the case insert slide tends to loosen

- The camming pin that slides in the case insert slide may get loose and need readjustment
- Most common problem–the case insert slide spring(13937) is broken or has weakened.[1e]

F–Upside down cases. There are three very common causes. First you should check for cases that got under the plate. This raises the plate and enables cases to hold upside down in the plate teeth. The second is excessive movement of the casefeeder hopper. Slow down or brace the hopper to the wall. The third is hard to believe, but this problem is more common when the hopper is getting low of cases.[4g]

6. Interruption of case and primer feed.

Frequently you need to stop the casefeeder or the primer feeder from continuing to function while you are making adjustments to dies and or powder charge.

A–Priming system. Here are several methods:[4h]

- A zip tie permanently attached to the failsafe bracket(secures the failsafe rod). The zip tie length is adjusted so it will loop around the primer arm and holds it back from advancing
- Remove the black plastic priming cam that the primer arm slides up, to advance the primers–this is my method

- A good video on youtube.com called "Dillon 650 Primer Feed Disable" shows how to use a tag washer(lobed flat washer) to disable the priming arm.
- Some reloaders do not bother with these methods and let the primers accumulate in the primer chute. When done with adjustments, they simply scoop them up and throw them back in the RF-100 or flip tray.[4h]

B–Casefeeder system.[4h]

This system has to be deactivated to make adjustments. A quick and simple method is to slip a 223 case behind the casefeed arm. This prevents the arm from picking up another case. I grind off the neck of the 223 case and slightly squeeze the case body for a ½ inch length along the bottle neck end of the case body.[4h] A youtube.com video showing this with a 357 mag case is "Dillon 650 Case Feed Mechanism Disable".

7. Humidity.[4i]

Humidity is the cause of rusting parts and needs to be controlled to maintain your presses. In the Xl 650 all steel parts are susceptible but the two worst are the steel pipe over the magazine tube and the steel roller arm of the main cycling system. In New England we don't have much of humidity problem but in Florida we do. In Florida I grease the main cycling arm and oil the magazine tube steel pipe and all steel parts.[4i]

For those who live in year round high humid climates where humidity is usually greater than 50%, more drastic measures may be beneficial. Those individuals generally protect the press with a Dillon zip up cover and insert a 20 watt bulb under cover–it works.[4i]

The other disadvantage to humidity is its effect on powder. Powder cannot sit in the hopper–you have to empty it when done reloading. The cover is not air tight and humidity will ruin the powder.

Humidity can cause problems with primers stored in their original cardboard boxes. I generally keep my primers year round in ziplock bags.

The only advantage to high humidity is that you don't have static problems with potential detonations–if that is a consolation!

8. Reloader's shoulder.

The older you are, the easier it is to develop fatigue and get sore joints especially the shoulder. Here are some helpful hints:[4j]

- Ignoring fatigue means you will end up with high primers or start making mistakes

- Changing the height of the press is usually beneficial. The higher the press, the easier it is to operate the main cycling arm by improving power leverage. The strong mount option achieves this edge
- Roller handle adds an ergonomic advantage
- Determine the length of your reloading session and stick to it
- Do not allow the press's capability be your stamina guide
- Use your body weight advantage while priming
- Consider trying to stand while reloading
- Add case lube even with pistol cases–especially 44 magnum and 45 long colt

In closing this chapter, look at the Blue Press monthly catalog again. This time look at every item on every page and read the descriptions of each item. I guarantee that you will be surprised. This catalog has all the Dillon products and many other popular shooting and reloading items. It also has new reloading/shooting articles each month.

OTHER PRESSES

Introduction

1. Single Stage Press

    A–Popular brands

    B–Dillon single stage

2. Turret Press

    A–Lyman press

    B–Lyman powder measure

    C–RCBS press

    D–RCBS powder measure

3. Progressive Press

    A–Transitional alternative–Lee turret

    B–Hornady AP press

    C–Hornady case feeder

    D–RCBS progressive Pro Chucker 5

    E–RCBS case feeder TUBE

4. Dillon Square Deal B

A–Blue press specifications

B–SDB manual–version 2009

C–Lubrication

D–Spare parts kit

E–Upgrades

F–FAQ'S

5. Chapter summary

Introduction.

Most reloaders started years ago with a single stage press. It is an ideal tool to learn the basics of reloading–one round at a time through each reloading die. This is usually done utilizing the "batch system"–where a lot of say +- 100 rounds are all sized/decapped/primed, then the lot gets powder charged and finally the lot goes through bullet seating/crimping.

Eventually the single stage press gets upgraded to a turret or progressive press. Yet the single press is still useful in the reloading room–for example.[6b]

- Decapping single or multiple cases
- Pulling bullets with a collet bullet puller or a "grip-on" puller(more on this tool later)
- Operating a GRX die(push-through sizing–more later)

- Sizing large rifle calibers
- Swaging crimped primer pockets
- Using a bullet pointing die
- Using a shoulder bump die
- Used with case forming dies[6b]

The switch from the single press to either a turret or a progressive press is based on many factors. These include preference, special uses, strength of hardware, versatility of tool and the need to produce a large volume of ammo per hour. Without a doubt, volume production of ammo is proportional to the need. Based on need, estimated production rates with a single stage is +- 100 rounds/hour for one month's shooting supply. When the need goes up to 200 rounds per month, the turret press would be a better choice with its production rate of 200 rounds per hour. If you need more than 300 rounds per month or have a busy schedule, it is time for a progressive press.[5a]

1. Single stage press

A–Popular brands[24]

- Lee reloader C press($34) and RCBS partner press($66)

These two are the basic and simple C shaped(easy access) presses for basic reloading or other uses mentioned above

- Lee challenger($66) or classic($117) breech lock and the Hornady Lock-N-Load($155) These are a step above the C press. They utilize a bushing system that allows you to lock a die in the bushing which can be replaced with another bushing/die without losing the dies zero settings–a great feature if these are your only press

- RCBS rock chucker supreme and the Redding Boss(both for +- $150). These are very strong classic single stage presses that will probably always be available. They are top quality, versatile and reliable.[24]

B–Dillon single stage. A Dillon XL 650 aftermarket variation produced by Uniquetek provides a conversion of the XL 650 to a single stage press. The conversion kit costs $95. This conversion allows you to keep reloading operations that simply cannot be done on a progressive press. It utilizes the press's main cyling arm and press linkage as there is no shellplate to flex. Therefore the force is directly over the center of the main cycling arm. Pictures and videos are available on their website uniquetek.com/product/.[26a]

2. Turret press

A–Lyman press($213)

The latest model is the T-Mag 2 turret–an upgraded version.[24]

- It has a movable turret handle for easy rotation
- The improved turret retention allows for smooth indexing while maintaining a solid support
- It has six stations and the turret is removable. A second turret can be substituted for other calibers for +- $49
- The compound leverage assures a powerful and smooth operation–as powerful as any heavy duty single stage press
- It comes with a complete priming system and spent primer catcher
- It cams over the shellholder thereby providing an excellent system for maximizing the sizing process. The overall strength of the unit makes it ideal for full length sizing even with extra large calibers
- A Lyman #55 powder measure is added to one station(see next page)
- It provides a C frame presentation for easy hand access[24]

Some reloaders who load one caliber with a three die set end up utilizing four stations–the fourth is the powder measure. Those who load two calibers on the same turret and use two die sets still only use 5 stations–the fifth is also the powder measure. I use my Lyman turret for full length sizing. I place the sizing/decapping die of four rifle calibers in my turret. I like the strength of this press to handle the difficult job of sizing rifle calibers(more details on this in later chapters). I am certain that many other setups are possible as well as special setups using extra turret heads.

The classic setup of this machine is as follows. Station 1 starts with a combination of sizing and priming. The second station is for the belling(M) die if needed. The third station is for the powder charge and the fourth station is for seating/crimping. If you use separate dies for seating and crimping you would use station four and five. Moving from one station is easy with a smooth action and a movable handle. The end result is a fully loaded round on every full manual cycle.

B–Lyman #55 Powder Measure($89).[24]

It is a smokeless powder measure only. It has a unique 3 slide adjustable cavity with an attached knocker that assures a consistent complete charge every time. A powder baffle in included in the hopper and a threaded adapter($10) attaches it to the turret head.[24]

A trick in setting the powder measure is to use the large cavity to approach the desired weight and finalize the adjustment by using the slide of the medium cavity. Rarely do you have to use the small slide.[13a]

C–RCBS turret press($190).[27]

The features of this press are very similar to the Lyman T-Mag–it is not surprising since the basic turret is all about the established industry standard. Like the Lyman, a second turret is available for $49. This machine is the same quality as the Lyman.[27]

It may seem difficult to improve the basic features of these two presses. One thing that could be changed is to add a bushing system like the Lee breech lock or the Hornady Lock-N-Load. This would allow one to change calibers without having to set each die separately again.

D–RCBS Uniflow powder measure($80).

This is also a smokeless powder measure. Unlike the Lyman #55 measure which uses the slide/drum system, this powder measure dispenses the charge from a measuring cylinder. It includes two drop tubes. A small that holds 0.5–50 grain and a large that holds 5–110 grains. Like the Lyman these powder measures handle all powders whether they are ball, flake or extruded.[27]

3. Progressive press

A–Transitional alternative–Lee turret.[24]

The Lee Classic 4 Hole Deluxe Kit($216) is a turret that automatically indexes and so can be classified as an economical progressive press. The kit also includes the following:

- Auto drum powder measure
- Second turret head available($15)
- Strong arm linkage for sizing rifle calibers
- Safety priming system
- Powder scale
- Case conditioning kit
- Revised Lee reloading manual–2nd edition
- Rated as +- 200 rounds per hour

The kit includes so many extras that a beginner only needs to purchase calipers, a square flip tray, dies, brass and loading components to get started–making this an extremely economical progressive press for beginners.[24] This press is also used by seasoned reloaders.

B–Hornady Lock-N-Load press($460).

This progressive press has many standard features as well as some unique qualities as follows:[28]

- Automatic indexing
- 5 station head
- Auto powder measure
- Lock-N-Load quick change bushing technology
- Comes with 5 bushings
- Capable of loading pistol and rifle
- Casefeeder available(section C)
- Priming system easily changed

- Case activated powder drop
- Quick change metering inserts for powder change
- Universal case retainer spring allows you to remove a case anywhere in the loading cycle
- Indexing is split–1/2 on the upstroke and 1/2 on the downstroke, makes for a smooth operation[28]

To complete this press you need to purchase a set of dies, a shellplate per caliber($34) and additional bushing as needed($10).[28]

Plan on extensive installation and fine tuning. There are no spare parts kit available but the press is covered with a lifetime warranty. Expect to call customer service for all parts.[12a]

C–Hornady Casefeeder($340).[28]

This is a perfect addition for the Lock-N-Load AP press. The features include:

- A high torque motor
- Extra large case bowl
- Quick change from one caliber to another
- Has six cartridge adapters to ensure proper feeding of cases into the shellplate
- Comes with extensive installation instructions[28]

There are two great videos on youtube.com for both the AP press and casefeeder. These make installation and fine tuning a much easier process. I would even suggest watching these videos before purchasing.

D–RCBS Pro Chucker 5($610).[24/27]

This is the most recent version of their progressive press and has similar features of both Dillon and Hornady with their own unique features:

- A 5 station auto indexing with a load rate of +- 600/ hour.
- Quick change die plate allows fast caliber change
- Safety shielded priming system
- Powder measure allows drainage without removing the measure from the press
- Quick change of powder metering tubes[24]

Like the other progressive presses, there are great videos on youtube on installation and operation of this press–also worth watching before purchasing. The Pro Chucker is the third design since 1970 and the jury is still out on this one.[12a]

E–RCBS Casefeeder tube)$150)[27]

The Pro Chucker does not have a powered casefeeder. Instead they have a tube thru which you manually have to add cases and repeatedly have to refill the tube. Their web site claims that Dillon and Hornady powered casefeeders can be retrofitted to the Pro Chucker. This requires extensive contact with RCBS customer service to order the parts needed and get some set up instructions.[27]

4. Dillon Square Deal B($400)

The Square Deal B is IMHO the most incredible engineering success that I had the pleasure of operating in the late 1970's. I loaded thousands of 38 special rounds and later my two teenage sons loaded innumerable rounds of 9mm. The machine functioned flawlessly without the need for frequent tweaking. Changing calibers was a simple five minute procedure.

This machine with its automatically indexing shellplate is intended to produce moderate quantities of match quality handgun ammo(straight wall cases only). Add a case and a bullet, pull the handle and a loaded round slides out into the bin.[3a]

A–Dillon Blue Press specs.

- Auto indexing
- Choice of 18 handgun calibers
- Production rate +- 400/hour
- Comes with one caliber conversion and complete die set
- Automatic powder measure

- Automatic priming system–includes two pickup tubes(L & S)
- Factory adjusted one caliber set of dies
- Lifetime no BS warranty
- 30 day free trial
- If needed, add an extra combination conversion/die set($88) and an extra toolhead($32)
- These are extras but strongly suggested:
- Pickup tubes, set of four(2 small & 2 large)($24) Spare parts kit($22)[3a]

Note–using a separate toolhead for each caliber allows you to change calibers without losing your die settings.[3a]

For the beginners, all you need to get started are a powder scale, reloading manual, calipers and a square flip tray. There are many setup and operational videos on youtube–but be reassured that this press has an easy and short learning curve.

B–SDB manual(2009 version)

Here are some helpful points found in the manual that are not always covered in videos.[3b]

Installation

- Make sure your bench is sturdy and does not shake. This may disturb your powder charge/priming system.

- Verify that the expander/powder funnel is free to move in the powder die
- When installing the failsafe rod, move the lock-link #17838 down to align the hole with the slot on the powder measure bellcrank #16814. The failsafe rod goes through these two holes. The other end of the failsafe rod is secured in place by inserting the failsafe rod clip #13840. Then adjust the failsafe rod with the operating handle forward, and adjust the wingnut till the spring is partially compressed. This may sound complicated but it is really simple and easily demonstrated in the youtube videos[3b]

Operation

- When the primer warning buzzer beeps, you are nearly out—only three primers remain in the system and it is time to refill
- After the seating depth is established, this depth adjustment is held in place by a layer of Delrin beneath the toolhead
- The crimp adjustment can be changed by screwing the adjustment screw up or down. Check the manual for crimp dimensions[3b]

C–Lubrication

Listed below are the lubrication points suggested by

Dillon. Go to youtube.com and follow along with the video "Lubricating the Dillon Precision Square Deal B". Use synthetic bearing grease and apply to:[3c]

- Link arms. Remove white washers, top and bottom, and remove the link arm. Grease inside and outside of link arm bearings and grease inside the holes of the link arm
- Crank handle pivot pin after loosening the set screw
- The underside of the shellplate bolt
- Vertical ribs, both front and back, of the connector bodycollar at the bottom of the powder measure
- Roller on the connector body collar of the powder measure
- Angled bottom edge of the index lever assembly(white plastic with spring)
- The inside of the roller bearing on the primer slide
- Clean the primer retaining pin hole with a pipe cleaner and alcohol. Lightly grease the head[3c]

D–Spare parts kit.

This is a great kit to have. It has 36 items for $22. In the kit are the parts that frequently need replacement because of metal fatigue or breakage. This kind of parts reserve will prevent you from closing down your reloading session to wait for parts. Here is a list of the very frequently used ones:[3a]

- Shellplate bolt
- 4 wave bearings
- Toolhead friction plate
- 2 decapping pins
- Slide return spring
- Bellcrank cube
- Indexer return spring
- 3/16 index ball
- 4 magazine orifices(2S and 2L)
- 2 retaining clips
- Index lever assembly[3a]

Note—As soon as I use a part, I place its replacement number and name in a holding list for the next order.

E–Upgrades.

There are SDB aftermarket upgrades available through e-bay and inlinefabrication.com.

Inlinefabrication[29a]

- LED light kit($29) that lights up the shellplate area
- Roller handle($48) that converts the wooden ball to a comfortable roller lever
- Bin barriers($4) that double the volume of the catch bin3
- Spent primer catcher($25). This does away with the stock primer cup and makes for a completely closed

system. No more primers on the floor and no more emptying of cup. The spent primer is collected in a container under the bench

• Strong mount($66), bullet tray($43) and powder knob. These three are the same as the ones on the XL 650

F–FAQ's

This section is usually popular because it covers the problems encountered by the users. Although the SDB is a trouble free machine, there are some situations that are recurring but can be corrected by the average reloader. As you check out the questions and answers, keep in mind that youtube has many videos that often deal with the same questions–so if the answer is not clear, go find a video. Most of the FAQ's were in the dillonprecision. com/forum[3d 1–20] web site and most of the answers were given by a Dillon customer service agent. The popular FAQ's were in five major categories and will be presented as such:

1. Primer feeding issues

   a. What causes a failure to prime?

      • Tight plastic tube end that holds primers from falling.
      • Wrong priming system.[3d]

b. Why is the primer slide not always loading?

- Measure the underside of the primer slide to the top of the primer cup. It should measure 1.410 in. If too tall because it loosened up–reset it. Use a clamp to reseat the cup/punch to the bottom of the slide and tighten the set screw.[3d1]

c. Why are multiple primers falling out?

- The primer retaining pin gets gummed up and it sticks rearward. This will drop multiple primers. Clean the hole in the housing, wipe off the pin and lightly grease the head end of the pin. The video on lubrication of the SDB shows this very well.[3d2-d3]

d. Why are primers flipping?

- This is a problem that can occur after years of use. The indexer tip(metal) has worn out and needs replacement. A simple solution when you watch the video on how to change it.[77]

e. What primers work best in the SDB?

- There are no restrictions to the use of any commercial primers. However CCI are a bit larger and harder and so they go in hard. This promotes high primers. For the primers that do not fall down the magazine tubes, add a 45 long colt cartridge to the end of the black follower rod to add weight to the follower rod.[3d4]

For persistent problems, check the ID of the tubes. The small tubes are .180 in. and the large are .210. If the ID is OK and the problem persists, then change your primer brand–you may have a primer concentricity problem or other primer defects.[3d5]

f. Why is the primer system jamming?

- The small orifice(blue) tip wears out and either the priming tube falls deeper or starts dropping extra primers–it needs changing.[3d6]

2. Sizing die issues.

a. What is the function of a friction plate?

→ There are 3 compression bumps molded in the underside of the blue friction plate. When they wear out, cases are failing to fully size. Pull the handle and the sizing die should touch the shellplate or it is time to change the friction plate.[25b/3d7]

b. Why are sized cases bulging?

- Sizing normally sizes the case tighter than the bullet diameter. This normally yields a bulge all the way around the case where the bullet base ends. This produces a visible ridge at the base of the bullet–which prevents bullet setback during chambering.[3d9]

c. How to remove a case stuck in sizing die?

- Remove the decapping assembly from the toolhead, then run a punch down through the sizing die's hole. Rap it with a hammer till the case falls out.[3d10]

3. Shellplate issues.

a. Why is the autoindexing faltering?

- Start looking at the shellplate bolt. It frequently breaks and often gets stuck in the platform upstroke. Try to catch it before it gets stuck.[3d11] A stuck shellplate is released by the method mentioned in 2c above.

b. What causes damage to a shellplate?

- Range brass has frequently been fired in oversize chambers. These cases get stuck in the sizing die and if you force the case out it will likely tear the case out of the shellplate and damage it.[3d12] Release the shellplate using the method in 2c.

c. Why is the shellplate rotating in the opposite direction?

- The shellplate detent ball spring is broken or the detent ball is gone—lost when you changed shellplates.[3d13]

4. Indexing issues.

a. Is there another cause for primers flipping?

- Take the press off the bench. In the bottom of the body is an indexing bolt. Take it out and grease it.[3d14]
- As mentioned, another cause of flipping or sideways primers is the indexer lever(metal tip) that has worn out. Usually there is a click in the action followed by flipping primers.[3d15] Refer back to #1d.

b. Why is the shellplate not indexing?

- The bolt in the bottom of the body, that holds the indexing finger, occasionally gets loose. Take the press off the bench to tighten it.[3d16]

c. Why is the shellplate turning rough and with resistance?

- The angled bottom of the index lever needs to be greased. Fortunately there is a video that shows how to do this on youtube.com.[3d17]

5. 9mm loading issues.

a. Why are cases getting stuck in the powder funnel?

- 9mm cases have a greater variation in case neck thickness which causes sticking. New brass needs "one shot" in the case mouth to prevent sticking.[3d18]

b. Why are cases bulging at the base?

- It is a common occurrence with 9 mm. If the loaded ammo passes a case gage, it will likely chamber. There is no pass through sizing dies made for the SDB.[3d19]

- Another cause of the bulging base is overloading the case to make a power factor. The SDB sizing die may not return the bulged cases back to normal without requiring an extra step on a separate press to run the cases in a GRX die.[3d19]

5. Chapter summary

Although I am a fervent user of Dillon equipment especially the XL 650, I have tried to present an unbiased approach to other presses. It is interesting to look at youtube videos on setup/problem solving of all presses and realize the frequency that these press videos are visited. The views were based on visits per year. The Hornady AP Lock-N-Load had +- 35,000 views, the RCBS Pro Chucker had +-20,000, the SDB had +-35,000 and the XL650 had +- 50,000.

You can interpret these statistics many different ways. Some people have purchased a press and are viewing the videos as a tutorial on setup. Others may be shopping and use the videos to help them decide which one to purchase. There are likely other interpretations but views may represent a reflection of interest, a practical need or a real demonstration of popular ownership.

CHAPTER-4

DILLON XL 650 UPGRADES

Introduction

1. HIT Factor bearing kit

2. Bullet feeders

   A–RCBS
   B–Hornady
   C–Mr. Bullet Feeder

3. Primer catchers

   A–Spent primer
   B–Live primer

4. Other miscellaneous

   A–Locator button tabs
   B–LED lighting
   C–Quick switch toolhead
   D–Powder slide knobs
   E–2X powder hopper
   F–Bin dam
   G–Micrometer powder bar

H–Powder measure drain

I– Casefeeder crud catcher

J–Dillon new index cam

Introduction.

Upgrades in the reloading world seem to belong to the after-market industry. Manufacturers appear to be adding to their product line or changing the inferior parts–leaving upgrades to the independent entrepreneur. Reloaders are often satisfied with the basic press and their listed accessories. Yet there is a group of reloaders who add after-market upgrades which often adds a new level of benefits. These upgrades not only add "bells and whistles" but can enhance ease of use. This is my popular list of upgrades for the Dillon XL 650.

1. HIT Factor bearing kit.

Many fast burning powders fill the case so much that when the shellplate indexes and stops past the detent ball– powder flips out of the case all over the work area. This is especially true with 9mm and the use of flake powders. Some old solutions include changing powders to Titegroup which is a fine powder with low volume. Another method is cutting 1/4 turn off the detent ball spring[78]. And finally adding the "o ring fix".[4m] Use a #2 locator pin and apply it to the chuck of a drill–which is fixed into a vise. Then apply a triangular file to the middle of the pin to create a groove as the pin is turning. Once the groove is formed, apply a #5 Danco o-ring(available at Home Depot). Finally apply the o-ring #2 pin back at station 4 or 5. The o-ring will now rub against the shellplate and dampen it. This o-ring fix is usually done with the detent spring cut 1/4 turn.

Note: there is a #2 locator pin in the spare parts kit.[4m]

The modern approach to fixing this Dillon powder flipping issue is the popular bearing kit. It includes a shellplate bearing washer, ball bearing camming pin and a low mass detent ball/spring. All these parts are easily installed with included instructions.[78]

The bearing washer allows you to tighten the shellplate bolt to max minus 1/8 turn. This rids the looseness of the shellplate as it now easily rides on the platform. The bearing camming pin reduces friction and smooths the reciprocating action of the case insert slide and slide cam.

The low mass detent ball/spring is a super hard but 7x lighter than a factory steel detent ball. It has less momentum when it locks up with the shellplate and absorbs vibrations better than a steel ball. Use the spring "as is" without cutting off 1/4 turn.[78]

With the addition of the bearing kit on top of the shellplate, the ejection wire is now three washers higher than it use to be.

This tends to jam the case on the wire and stop the press. The instructions show the proper way to bend the ejection wire to make it functional.[2a]

I have installed this kit and I am amazed to see its advantages–the shellplate indexing is so smooth! I strongly recommend its use.

2. Bullet feeders. The new age of big upgrades includes bullet feeders. I have been following their development for years and can finally mention three that may have a niche with seasoned reloaders. These machines require a mechanical finesse and years of loading experience. They are not for the beginner reloader.

A–RCBS. Pisol($430) and Rifle($485)

This bullet feeder can be adapted to most progressive presses but it fits best on the RCBS Pro Chucker. It only loads jacketed bullets–no lead cast bullets. Does all pistol calibers except for 44 Magnum. It comes with a two year warranty. Information seems skimpy from the manufacturer and many retail web sites.[24/27] I finally had to resort to reading many forums on this subject–only to find this consensus":

- This feeder does not adapt well to other presses
- Bullet feeding fingers are not durable and easily break
- Cases must be excessively belled for proper operation

- The feeder will not keep up with the progressive press since the sorting wheel may turn 20X before dropping a bullet
- Too many potential problems and too many parts to keep in inventory

These negative comments may reflect personal opinions that are hard to interpret. All forums agreed that this bullet feeder should be used with RCBS presses–that is what it was designed for. Also the forums agreed that customer service was very good for replacement parts and they made the fine adjustments easier to manage.[24/27]

B–Hornady. Pistol($278) Rifle($383 for 22cal) ($512 for 30 cal.) The listed features of this feeder include:[17/24]

- Can be fitted to other presses but it works best with Hornady
- This feeder can handle jacketed, plated bullets. It can also handle lead bullets with some necessary modifications
- It comes with a lifetime warranty
- Must use Hornady bullet feeder dies for each pistol caliber

It appears that all bullet feeders are finicky and actually require patience and finesse in using these products. It would also be wise to fit your bullet feeder to the same brand of progressive press. After reviewing forums and retail catalogs, I went to youtube and found many videos on both the RCBS and Hornady bullet feeders. If you have either of these presses and are considering a bullet feeder, check out the videos. You will be surprised!

C–Mr. Bullet Feeder($470 plus $150 per caliber conversion). We finally have a bullet feeder that can easily fit the Dillon Xl 650. It is well presented in the Blue Press catalog since 2017. This is likely the best performing personal-use bullet feeder on the market since 2006. Double-Alpha academy has teamed up with RAK systems to redesign and make it more compact, versatile and more affordable.[87]

Here are the features of this bullet feeder:[1a/31/87]

- The bullet collator can be mounted onto the casefeeder thereby not affecting bench space use
- Web site(mrbulletfeeder.com) provides eight "how to videos"
- Can use jacketed, plated or coated bullets
- Finally can use lead cast bullets. If the lead bullets are moly coated, no modifications are needed–very important
- If using hard wax lube on lead bullets, modifications are needed. The plate and dropper tube need to be cleaned often when they get sticky. A light coating

of mica on the bullets will decrease wax build up and decrease need for cleaning. Reloading in a cool environment will also decrease need of cleaning

- In the Dillon XL 650, this bullet feeder needs its own station to deliver a bullet. This means you have to use a combined seater/crimping die or remove the powder check system
- This feeder also fits on RCBS and Hornady presses
- Will not handle wad-cutter type bullets–SWC are OK
- The special powder funnel gives proper flare to hold the bullet
- The dropper works, bullets fall when three balls are retracted by pushing the unit down. Ingenious and simple. Need to watch the videos to understand the drop mechanism
- Buy it from Dillon because of great customer service.[1a/31/87]

Forum reviews revealed more information. This bullet feeder consists of a motorized collator plate, mounting spacers for the casefeeder, spring tube, powder funnel/case mouth expander, bullet dropper, variable speed switch and spare ball bearings.[79] Others include:

- The bullet dropper has an electro mechanical switch that is wired to the collator and shuts it off when the dropper is full
- If bullets fall into the holes upside down, the collator will rotate the bullets then allows them to slide down the spring tube to the dropper
- Length of bullets is adjusted with spacers for the collator
- The other installation is the powder funnel expander–replaces the Dillon product.[79]
- IMHO, why would you consider a bullet feeder?
- Need to increase production because of shooting sports
- Limited reloading time because of employment
- Arthritic problems with hands or shoulder
- Amputee disability
- Ample videos for installation and operation
- Addicted to more bells and whistles
- Price finally in "affordable" range
- I always wanted one!
- Use of Dillon customer service cancels any reservations about an advanced mechanical instrument

In summary, adding a bullet feeder to a combination progressive press/casefeeder is basically creating an ammo producing factory. WOW all you have to do is to run the cycling/priming arm to produce a loaded round. However you have to watch, listen and be alert–you are operating an advanced machine with many working parts.

The Mr. Bullet Feeder is a highly acclaimed smooth operating machine relatively free of the need for "fixes". I suspect that many seasoned reloaders have been waiting for affordability and ability to handle lead bullets. IMHO this bullet feeder is the ultimate upgrade for the practical reloader using a Dillon XL 650 and other presses.

3. Primer catchers

A–Spent primers($25). The Dillon XL 650 has a habit of spitting spent primers out of the plastic receptacle. This primer catcher is a simple tube that transfers the spent primer into a bottle away from the press via a closed system. Finally no more spent primers on the floor. Available on e-bay.[1f]

B–Live primers($20). This resolves the problem of missed live primers flying off the primer chute. The primer catching chute funnel primers into a plastic bottle which can be removed to reuse the primers. Again, no more lost good primers on the floor. Also available on e-bay.[1f]

4. Other Upgrades.

A–Locator button tabs. It is unclear why Dillon no longer

makes these tabs available. Since I reload three pistol calibers, I move the old tabs from one caliber to another. You can make your own out of plastic ties that are perforated to fit the locator buttons. They are also available on e-bay($5).[1f]

B–LED lighting($39). An Inline-Fabrication product which produces a high output LED pod installed into the center hole of the toolhead. It perfectly lights up the entire work area without being visually offensive since the light is shining downward. It also includes a 4 inch LED strip that attaches to the inside press frameif you need the extra light beyond the dome unit. Caliber changes are easy since you pop it out of the toolhead and exchange it. It comes with a 110 adapter, a 4 foot long cord, on/off switch and wire routing anchors.[29b]

C–Quick switch toolhead kit($60). This kit converts "special to magnum" cases such as 38 special/357 mag or 44 special/magnum. A product of Ultimate Reloader, that features a flip-able spacer that adjusts the toolhead to compensate for the difference in case length between special and magnum cases–as long as you are using the same bullet. Otherwise you have to adjust the seating die but never have to adjust the other dies. Also available on e-bay.[41]

D–Powder slide knobs($2). A plastic knob that fits on the 7/16 nut and allows you to change the powder charge by using your fingers instead of a wrench. Available on e-bay.[30]

E–2X Powder hopper($38). A product of Uniquetek that

measures 14 inches and includes a powder baffle–this easily exchanges with the standard hopper. The extra feature is that this clear plastic does not stain with extended powder contact.[26b]

F–Bin dam($6). Another Uniquetek product that provides a plastic barrier to double the size of the catch bin.[26b]

G–Micrometer powder bar($80). A Uniquetek product that replaces the original 1/4–28 thread adjustment bolt with a micrometer of 40 threads/inch. It allows you to return instantly to any recorded powder setting without guessing how many turns needed on the bolt.

H–Powder measure drain($18). A Uniquetek product that allows users to drain the powder hopper without removing the powder measure off the powder die. Very handy when you need to change the powder, powder bar or drain the hopper at the end of a reloading session.[26b]

I–Casefeeder crud catcher($19). The casefeeder has two holes in the bottom of the bowl that allows media to clear out of the bowl–all over your reloading bench! This catcher provides two tubes that attach to the holes and directs the media into a container.[26b]

J–Dillon new index cam. The index ring rotates the shellplate by sliding over the index cam. This index cam has recently been improved by making it 0.120 inch taller. This change increases the time between when the shellplate has completed its index and when the primer punch starts up through the shellplate. This is to prevent the primer punch coming in contact with the bottom of the shellplate–the result would be primers flipping upside down. Available through Dillon customer service.

In closing this chapter, upgrades seem to come in two sizes–big and small. The two big ones are Mr. Bullet Feeder and the HIT Factor Kit. However, the long list of small and cheaper upgrades seem to make the use of my XL 650 so much more pleasant. I hope that our manufacturers, inventors and entrepreneurs come out with more useful upgrades. My wish list includes an automation system for the XL 650–with or without computer controls!

RELOADING ACCESSORIES

Introduction

1. Bullet puller

    A–Kinetic hammer

    B–Grip-N-Pull

    C–RCBS bullet puller die

    D–Hornady cam lock die

2. Tumblers

    A–Why tumble

    B–Types-vibratory, rotary, ultrasonic

3. Media

    A–Types

    B–Powdered polish

    C–Liquid polish

    D–Decapping

4. Case handling

    A–Media separators

B–Brass collectors

C–Shell sorters

5. Scales

A–Balance beam vs. electronic scales.

B–Product brands

C–Powder dispenser/scale combo

D–Powder tricklers

6. Trimmer

A–Why trim

B–Manual

C–Powered

D–Dillon auto size/trim

7. Chronograph

A–Definition/purpose

B–Basic unit

C–Advanced technology

8. Brass catchers

A–Bench anchor

B–Tripod field anchor

C–Hand held

D–Ground tarp

9. Gun rests

    A–Basic pistol
    B–Advanced pistol
    C–Basic rifle
    D–Magnum rifle

10. Case lube

    A–Hornady one shot
    B–Dillon case lube
    C–Removing case lube
    D–Other products
    E–Case denting

11. Stuck cases

    A–Cause
    B–How it works and products
    C–Dillon die method

12. Gages

    A–Case length gages
    B–Headspace gages
    C–Calipers

13. Case prep tools

    A–Basic/manual
    B–Powered centers
       –Hornady case prep Duo and Trio
       –RCBS trim mate center
       –Lyman case prep center

14. Swage tools

    A–Manual and powered
    B–Single stage press units
    C–Super swagers

15. Shellholders

16. Primer tube holders

Introduction.

Once you take the step to become a reloader, you need to choose the press with one caliber conversion, dies, cases, powder, primers and bullets. On the surface it would seem that this is all you should need! Well it is time you realized that more is needed on a reloading bench to produce ammo. Certain basic accessories are needed in the process of reloading. These include a case tumbler, tumbler media, case polish, case lube, media separator, powder scale, square primer flip tray, reloading manual, calipers and a bullet puller.[6c]

You are now realizing that reloading ammo is not a "one time" weekend event—it is a long term investment in a practical hobby that uses many tools of the trade. This chapter will discuss these ten necessary items and many other optional ones.

1. Bullet puller.

A—Kinetic hammer($20). A simple tool that holds a completed round by the rim and upon impact on a hard wood surface, the bullet and powder fall out of the case. Remember to put foam at the bottom of the cavity to catch pointed bullets and avoid deforming them. This tool is ideal for dismantling an occasional bad round or a semi wadcutter since there are no settings to be adjusted—it is used "as is" as long as you match the proper retaining ring(choice of three) to the diameter of the case.[24] The violent nature of the kinetic hammer does sometimes disrupt the anvil and so I save these primed cases for practice loads. I have built an impact site—an 18 inch hardwood 2X4 with stabilizing legs. Instead of hitting the hammer on my reloading bench, this impacting bench sits on the floor—the impact does not disrupt any of the sensitive tools on my reloading bench.

B–Grip-N-Pull($40 each for pistol and rifle). This is a specialized plier that holds the bullet while the single stage press pulls the case off the bullet. This is a smooth operation that does not potentially disrupt the primer anvil–allowing reuse of the primed case without decapping the case. This die uses a collet specific for each caliber. This system is ideal for lead bullets(excluding semi wadcutters) and works best with jacketed bullets but is also used with coated bullets. It works on a standard single stage press–place a loaded round in the press, lift up the ram, then tighten the collet. On lowering the ram, the bullet is removed. Another economical system for dismantling large batches of ammo.[24/27/5b]

Whether you can use this system on plated bullets depends on the bullet manufacturer and your own experience.

D–Hornady cam-lock bullet puller($26 plus $12 for each collet). This system is very similar to the RCBS puller except the collet has a quick cam that clamps the collet to the bullet.[24/17]

2. Tumblers.

A–Why tumble cases. Tumbling cases removes dirt, grit and powder fouling plus it polishes the cases. This reduces the chances of damaging dies and certainly makes resizing a much easier process. Clean cases makes spotting cracks easier. The bottom line, reloaders generally process their cases in a tumbler–it may also be a matter of pride. No one wants to go to a range or a competition and come out with dirty fouled cases![2b]

B–Vibratory. The many features are secondary to matching a tumbler to your needs. IMHO, a tumbler needs to handle the number of cases that you usually reload during a typical reloading session. I empirically add 100 more cases to the batch. In my situation, my reloading session usually involves 600 rounds and so my tumbler(Lyman 2500 pro magnum) can handle 700–38 or 9mm cases. The proper recipe to maintain a cascading of the tumbler's media is to fill your tumbler with 75% media and then add your minimum number of cases to match your reloading session–plus some extras. Other tumbler features which may fit your needs include:

- Lid sifter. Not to be used if you use a powdered polishing agent. Always best to use a separate media separator
- Motor thermally protected
- Autoflow of questionable value
- Adequate suspension to decrease noise
- Adequate vibrating action to promote "cascading"
- If need a second bowl, get it from the manufacturer. Twin bowls are not a great idea since the second bowl is half size
- All day use requires a motor that turns on precision ball bearings

These are some examples of vibratory tumblers that denote the number of 38 cases it can handle from large to small:[2b]

- Dillon CV-2001($190) #1300–38. Largest in the industry with a 12.5 qt. bowl. Motor is internally cooled, thermally protected and turns on precision ball bearings. The bowl is 7/32" thick of high strength polypropylene
- Lyman 2500 Pro magnum($85) #1000–38
- RCBS Large($99) #800–38 plus a small unit($89) #400–38
- Dillon CV-750($145) #650–38. Same motor as the CV-2001
- Hornady M-2($90) #500–38.
- Frankford Arsenal($50) #500–38.
- Lyman turbo($60) #350–38.[2b]

C–Rotary. The sideways rotating action polishes as well as a vibratory tumbler but does clean cases better than a vibratory unit Here are two examples. The Lyman Cyclone rotary tumbler($186) can handle 1000–223 cases and has a lined bowl for quiet tumbling. Although it can work with dry media, it works best with stainless steel pins and a cleaning solution. The latter would add a separate drying cycle.[2c/24]

The other unit, The Thumbler's tumbler model B($195), follows the industry standard and is basically similar the the Lyman Cyclone. Again a steel hexagon barrel with a rubber lining that rotates at 40 rpm and works best with stainless steel pins/liquid media.[2c/24]

D–Ultrasonic cleaners. These work by producing high frequency vibrations that blast away at case's carbon residue, tarnish and oxidation changes. They clean cases inside and out very well but they DO NOT POLISH. They can also be used to clean gun parts.[2c/24] In comparing Lyman, RCBS and Hornady, there seems to be an industry standard that they all conform to. This is the RCBS ultrasonic cleaner-1($140). It has a 60 watt transducer with a 100 watt ceramic heater. It has a "degas" function that removes gas from the cleaning solutions.[32] The tank capacity is 3.2 qt. and it handles +- 400–223 cases. These specifications are very similar for the Lyman Turbo Sonic cleaner($114) and the Hornady Lock-N-Load 2L($100).[2c/24]

All these sonic cleaners use a cleaning solution specific for this cleaner. An example is the Hornady One Shot sonic cleaning solution($60 per gallon) but good for +- 200 cleaning cycles depending on how dirty the cases are. Whenever using a sonic cleaning solution, verify that it can be used with nickel plated cases since they tend to turn these cases black. As with rotary tumblers, a drying cycle is necessary.

3. Media.

A–Types. There are two basic dry medias–corn and walnut. Corn is great for polishing cases while cleaning them. Walnut is best for cleaning cases while providing a low luster brushed finish. Walnut is a harder material and so lasts longer. You generally can get +-15 runs with a dry media before recharging or changing it.[33]

The time to change or recharge your media is when it takes more than 2 hours to process a full batch of cases. Some prefer to recharge their worn out media by replacing 1/3 of the media with new media and adding polish. It is also common practice to periodically add more polish as a stop-gap recharging method.[33] Some reloaders like to have the advantage of both media by mixing the two in equal parts.[6d]

B–Powdered polish. There are two commonly used dry powders–red rouge and RCBS. Red rouge is commonly called "jewelers rouge" and it is a compound of Iron Oxide. Red rouge is available thru MLS manufacturing or at brasstumblers. com/brass-polish. It comes in a tub at ($22) per pound and can be added to corn or walnut. It has a hardness level of 6 on the Mohs hardness scale and is perfect for soft metals such as brass. It only takes a very small amount to add a red tinge to your media and increase the abrasive action of your media.[12c] A commercial preparation that already has red rouge added to walnut is the Lyman "Tuffnut".[24]

The RCBS white polishing powder is my personal choice. It comes in packets of five bags and generally each bag will handle 7–8 pounds of corn media. I order my corn media through Frankford arsenal and add half of a 15 pound bag into my Lyman 2500 tumbler. As new media, I add two bags of powder and run the tumbler for 5 minutes. When I recharge the media, I only add one bag at a time.[24/17]

Polishing powders can produce more tumbling dust than liquid polish. This is usually managed by letting the tumbler settle before pouring out the contents, using an exhaust fan or using laundry anti-static sheets. The latter may hasten the failure of your polishing powder by absorbing not only tumbling dust but by absorbing some of the polishing compound.

C–Liquid polish. It is also a good polishing method and many industry preparations are available to include Lyman's Turbo Brite polish, Midway brass polish, Dillon's Rapid Polish 290 and many others. The problem with all liquid polish is the "how much to use" directions. It generally states to add several cap-fulls to the media. Is that two or three or four cap-fulls? Well you have to experiment and will generally ruin one batch of corn media from adding too much polish–clumping the corn out of use. There are many other polishing agents that can be used in corn or walnut media to include automotive waxes such as NuFinish car polish and Turtle wax. Look at the contents of all polishing agents and avoid the ones that contain ammonia which promotes cracked cases.[2d] In addition to these additive polishes, there are many media choices that have the proper amount of liquid polish already added.

D–Decapping. For the general reloader, IMHO decapping cases before tumbling serves no practical advantages–this is a common technique with benchrest shooters. Vibratory and rotary tumblers do not clean primer pockets well–ultrasonic cleaners do. The media gets stuck in the flash hole and may create problems. If you are the type that insists on decapping before tumbling, then use pet store "lizard litter" which is ground smaller than standard media and falls freely from primer pocket flash holes.[2e]

4. Case handling.

A–Media separators. These generally include a manual sifter and a rotary type. A simple manual sifter is available through Frankford Arsenal that measures a 4 inch high straight wall with a hole diameter of .270". The action involves transferring the media/cases back and forth between the sifter and a solid pan–over a bucket. The media falls in the bucket and the cases remain in the sifter.[24]

The rotary type involves a squirrel cage rotating over a collecting tub–which effectively separates the media from the cases. These are some of the popular ones:[2f/24]

- Dillon CM-2000($76). A large 10"X14" cage over a 18"X22" tub. It can hold 1500–223 cases
- Dillon CM-500($48). Holds half the capacity of the CM-2000
- RCBS rotary case separator($37). It is smaller than the CM-500 and handles 400–38 cases.[2f/24]

B–Brass collectors. Picking up brass off the ground is a boring and tedious process. Several companies(Battenfield, Caldwell, Dillon and Uniquetek) now make a screened roller that picks up brass($24–48).

Simply roll over the brass and it gathers over concrete, gravel, sand and grass. The end caps open to empty the collected brass and the handle is a telescoping 28–57". It generally holds +-50 pistol or +-25 rifle cases before it needs to be emptied out.[2g] The alternative to this tool is a basic tarp on the ground to collect your brass–not always easy to do in a public range.

C–Shell sorter. When you pick up range brass with a "roller collector" you usually end up with unwanted calibers. By sorting out the calibers before tumbling, you avoid smaller cases that get stuck in larger cases. This plastic sorter($42), also available through Dillon, comprises of three pans with different size of slots. Place all three pans over a bucket with the black pan in the bottom, the blue one in the middle and the yellow one on top. The yellow sorts 45acp, 44 sp/mag, and 45 colt. The blue sorts 40 S&W, 10mm, and 38/357. The black sorts 9mm and 380acp. Uniquetek.com makes an aluminum pan($22) that separates 380acp from 9mm.[2g]

5. Scales.

A–Balance beam vs. digital electronic scales. Irrelevant of the press you are using, you need to verify that the intended powder charge is confirmed by a scale. The real issue with scales is the pros and cons of electronic vs. balance beam scales.[34a]

- With any electronic equipment, longevity may be an issue whereas a balance beam scale lasts a lifetime
- Electronic scales drift with temperature and electronic interference from phones, routers and laptop computers
- Electronic ones are poor for repeated weighing since you have to hit the "tare" button on each one
- Cheap electronic ones are not accurate
- Electronic ones are great for weighing brass and bullets. A practice common with benchrest shooters
- Buy electronic scales with batteries. You can use them at the range and you can pull the batteries when not in use or get the ones with auto disconnect when not in use to save the batteries

- Start electronic scales ahead–need a warm up period
- Some can weigh up to 1/100 grain–great for benchrest shooters
- Electronic scales are sensitive equipment–don't drop them![34a]

Balance beam scales are my choice and do not require a warm up period or calibration once zero is set on your bench. They are quick and less sensitive to air currents or temperature fluctuations. The balance beam only weighs to 1/10 grain which is acceptable to non benchrest shooters. They simply seem to be reliable from day to day.[13b/16a]

B–Product brands. These are the popular balance beams:

1–RCBS 500($68).

- Alloy frame with aluminum pan
- Adjusts to 0.1 gr. and a maximum measure of 511 grains
- Wheel adjustment to set scale to zero
- It has magnetic dampening to better settle the measurements
- The main beam is in 5 grain increments, the fine adjustments are in 1 grain and extra fine settings in 1/10 grains.[35a]

2–Redding #2($85). Similar features as #1 but has a steel frame.[35a]

3–Hornady($80). Similar features as #1.[24]

4–Dillon eliminator scale($80). Similar features as #1.[2i]

These are the popular electronic scales:

1–Dillon Terminator electronic scales($140).[2i]

- 1500 grain capacity
- Accuracy at 0.1 gr
- Uses 4 AA batteries or an AC adapter
- Scale check weight included
- LCD display
- Dust cover available($15)
- One year warranty.[2i]

2–RCBS range master 2000($120).[24]

- Touch screen operation
- Battery saving auto shut-off
- Uses 9 volt battery or an AC adapter
- 2000 grain capacity with similar 0.1 gr. accuracy
- Dust cover included
- Other features similar to Dillon Terminator.[24]

C–Powder dispenser/scale combo.

1–RCBS Chargemaster($350). This is a combination of the 1500 powder scale and the chargemaster powder dispenser. It works this way: Fill hopper with one pound of smokeless powder, enter the desired charge and press dispense. The average dispensing time is 30 seconds for +-60 grains. It works with extruded, ball and flake powders. The cover over the pan eliminates air current fluctuations in the powder charge. It is mentioned in this section only to emphasize that this advanced dispenser is not really made for the volume reloader– it is more a tool for the handloading benchrest shooter.[24]

D–Powder tricklers. This is an inexpensive way to dispense a very accurate powder charge. Place a standard powder charge of say 50 grains on an electronic scale and then trickle minute amounts of the same powder to reach 50.7 grains. The RCBS trickler($24) is made of cast aluminum with a non skid stable base. It has a powder tube extension to reach a pan of electronic scales that is out of reach. The trickler works well with a powder dispenser/scale of benchrest shooters.[24]

6. Trimmers.

A–Why trim rifle cases. With repeated reloading of rifle cases, the case lengthens. If the case is left too long, the mouth may get crimped onto the bullet which will then cause the bullet to be held by the barrel chamber–delaying the bullet release and leading to excessive pressures.

All calibers have a maximum case length–any length beyond this should be trimmed. The case length minimum is the "trim to length" as noted in your reloading manual. The difference in minimum and maximum case length is usually 0.10 in. unless otherwise specified in the reloading manual. The best time to measure your cases is after sizing–that is when the case necks have elongated.[12d] Of note, we generally do not trim pistol cases–possibly with the exception of hot 44 magnum loads.

B–Manual trimmers.[24]

1–RCBS Trim Pro-2($90).

- Fewer manual turns needed to trim
- Universal spring loaded lever shellholder eliminates need to purchase separate trimmer plates
- Uses standard pilots–9 included
- Trimmer will hold cases with rim diameters of .250" to .625"
- Die cast metal with hardened cutting blades.

2–Lyman universal carbide case trimmer ($109). Features very similar to the RCBS Trim Pro above.

C–Power trimmers.

1–Lyman Universal trimmer/power pack combo($98). This is a manual trimmer with a conversion shaft that utilizes a standard drill as a power source–change the manual standard shaft with handle to a power shaft and apply the drill. It comes with a universal shellholder and 9 pilots. This is a real economical trimmer since it is all inclusive and no other parts are needed. An upgrade carbide cutter head is available for $41.[24]

2–Hornady Cam-lock trimmer kit($80). The features are similar to #1 above. However it uses caliber specific shellholders to hold the case. It also has a high frame that prevents knuckle busting and a power drill can be attached.[24]

3–Lyman Universal power trimmer($375). This unit has its own power source. It is powered by a 175 RPM motor to add speed to the process. It comes with the usual 9 pilots and it uses the universal shell-holder mechanism of standard trimmers.[24]

4–RCBS Trim Pro-2($250). This has very similar features as #3 above. This is also an all inclusive system with the pilots and universal shellholder. This is a hands free operation since the spring fed cutter requires no pushing or feeding. An economical choice.[24/27]

D–Dillon auto size/trim($331). The Rapid Trim 1500 uses individual caliber sizing/trim dies($60 each caliber). While you push the the case in the sizing die, an electric motor is driving a carbide cutter at 4500 RPM and trims the case to length as set. Trimming chips are drawn off through a vacuum manifold that clamps to the outside of this special size/trim die. This unit can be used on any brand of press to include both single stage and progressive presses. I you size and decap on another press, this unit can be used solely as a trimmer when placed on any press. It is certainly a major upgrade in trimmers and has its own niche with precision handloaders that deal with large amount of cases such as benchrest shooters or similar groups. The price keeps it out of reach for the practical volume reloader that only has small batches of hunting rifle cases to trim.[2j]

7. Chronographs.

A–Definition and purpose. A chronograph uses two screens that sense the shadows of passing bullets and converts the passing times into velocity. The result is a velocity determination that provides verification of an intended velocity. Other features include:[9a]

- This is essential if you compete and need to confirm your required power factor minimum as in USPSA
- If you compete with cast bullets in CAS, you need to confirm your high and low velocity limit. It is important with trajectory charts that require a correct velocity

- Published data in manuals can differ greatly when used in "your specific pistol". Avoid a surprise on the chrono test at competition registration!
- Chronographs are finicky. They are affected by light, clouds, sun, heat, cold, wind and time of day. You almost have to try to duplicate the environment from one shooting session to the next.[9a]

B–Basic unit. An example of a standard unit is the "Competition Electronics pro chrono digital chronograph"($110). This unit features:[24]

- Measures velocities between 22 and 7000fps
- Records 9 strings of fire and computes statistics for each string to include high, low, average number of shots, standard deviations and extreme spread
- Can download statistical info to a PC via a "hyper terminal"(a component of Microsoft windows)
- Allows the unit to be operated remotely via a 20 ft. cable
- Has a mounting hole thread for a 1/4 X 20 mount
- The "brains" of the unit are in line with the shooter–just below the sensors. Operated by a 9 volt battery.[24]

Other units by Shooting Chrony, Pact and others have similar features in the same price range. For the volume reloader that competes, this grade of chronographs certainly can fit their needs.

C–Advanced technology chronographs. An example of this technology is the "CED Millennium-2 Chrono"($200). Its features include:[2k/24]

- Advanced software and digital circuitry for fast performance
- Records velocity from 50 to 7000fps
- Readings to include high, low, average and high average
- Has a built-in calculator
- Power factor computation function for IPSC/IDPA
- Has voice chip technology
- Has an auto shutdown mode
- PC download capability–USB interface for software download of stored data. Data collection software included
- It also includes support arms, sun screen, sensors, main unit, large display and keypad, mounting bar/base and DVD user guide
- Main unit is away from sensors(not in line of shooter)
- Has a wireless connection from the sensors to the box
- Optional–soft carrying case for unit and battery pack.[2k/24]

There are many other units with a similar price range and features. These include Shooting Chrony, Pact, Caldwell and others. IMHO these advanced chronographs are likely better suited for the benchrest and long range precision shooters.

8. Brass catchers.

A–Bench anchor. CTK Precision Universal brass catcher($60). This unit sits on the bench next to the firearm. It is a steel frame and mesh net that has an opening of 16"X16" and stands 19 inches high.[24]

B–Tripod field anchor. "Brass Trap"($40) can be used on a bench or on a tripod with a 1/4 X 20 thread. The mesh is heat resistant and has a zippered bottom for easy emptying. The unit collapses to fit in a range bag. This type of brass catcher allows you to stand and shoot freestyle because the catcher is on an adjustable tripod to match your height. It also follows you if you vary your target yardage.[24]

C–Hand held brass catchers($25). These are used on auto pistols for shooting freestyle–the key is to find one that fits your pistol.[24]

D–Tarp. This is the most economical way to collect your brass. A 6 X 6 ft. tarp with corner weights will keep most of your brass in one place. This is not always feasible at a public range–in this case a tripod as mentioned in B above works quite well.

9. Gun rests.

A–Basic pistol. Any basic pistol rest($25) from MTM or Caldwell and others, includes a barrel rest, a platform for the grip and often have elevation adjustments. These are used when establishing accuracy for a specific firearm and load. More sophisticated types are available such as the "HySkore pivoting pistol rest"($50). It has height adjustments, 150 degree rotation for windage, locking levers, spirit level, foam padded platform and anchor points for bench stabilization.[24]

B–Advanced pistol. The "Ransom Rest" has become an international standard for accuracy testing. It holds, fires and recoils a handgun–providing a fixed gun for reliable testing. The "Ransom Master"($414) comes with grip inserts for your gun to hold it firm and precisely. The recoil is handled by the grip inserts($55 each) and the designed mechanism which breaks each shot in an identical manner. It can handle recoil up to and include 44 magnum. All grip inserts are attached to the rest by the ABC plate that is retained by three star knobs. For more info go to their web site: ransomrest.com/home/master-series.[24]

C–Basic rifle. An economical rifle rest "Caldwell Zero Max rest"($33) provides full windage and elevation adjustment. The medium filled front bag provides a rock solid shooting base. An example of more options includes the MTM Case-Gard Predator rest($40). This one includes the usual elevation/

windage adjustments plus adjusts to fit long guns. The central body twists for 4 point contact. It holds front and rear bags and can be used as a handgun rest with the rear support removed.[24]

I have a rifle/pistol combo rest from "Inventive Technology". It includes two Y shaped rubber yolks that are elevation adjustable. The pistol platform is removable and fits behind the front yolk. In either mode, it provides a stable rest and is very portable–although it is 30 years old, the model is still available today with some modifications. It is available at sharpshooterhq. com under the name of "Sharp Shooter rifle rest"($75).

D–Magnum rifle. With the advent of so many magnum rifles, is the welcome arrival of the "lead sled". Caldwell Lead Sled 3($120) is a recoil reducing rifle rest. It is ideal for hot rifle loads, magnum loads or extended rifle shooting episodes. The sled holds 25 lb. bags of lead shot. Recoil shock absorbing pads and the rear cradle cushions the firearm. This new use of lead shot bags to absorb recoil can significantly reduce felt recoil.[24] IMHO, despite the use of lead shot, some shooters remove the rear cradle to prevent the disputed possibility of scope damage and use a Past shoulder pad to cushion recoil.

10. Case lube.

Whenever you size rifle and some large pistol cases, you

need to lubricate the cases–a mandatory process. The issue is to choose the ideal lubricant for the job at hand.

A–Hornady one shot. This is a non sticky, non petroleum based lubricant in an aerosol that dries to a dry film. It is available in a 5 oz.($10) or a 10oz.($14) can. Use the black top can labeled case lube–not the dry lube. The key to proper use is to shake it vigorously before use and then spray the cases. Place cases in a loading tray and spray on both sides of the cases as well as 45° into the case mouth–does not affect powder. Spraying into the case mouth facilitates sizing/release from the internal neck mandrel and also eases release from the powder funnel. It is very important to let the sprayed cases thoroughly dry for 10 minutes or more–to obtain the dry lubricating film before sizing them.[2l/2m/28a]

I have used this lubricant in short/medium rifle cases such as 308, 243, 30-30, 7mm-08 and it has performed well without stuck cases. I always use it in long pistol cases such as 44 magnum. It is an ideal lubricant if you are only neck sizing.

The real user friendly aspect of this dry lube is the fact that it does not have to be removed from the loaded round.[28a]

B–Dillon case lube(DCL). A mixture of alcohol(5) to lanolin(1) comes in 8oz. for $9. This is my "go-to" lubricant for all rifle cases–especially the long cases such as 270, 30-06 and others. Spray the cases using the method in A above.

Allow the alcohol to evaporate and it leaves an oily film of lanolin on the cases.[21/28a]

C–Remove case lube. After the rounds are loaded, the DCL oily film has to be removed. This is easily done by tumbling them in a plain corn media with one tablespoon of alcohol or mineral spirits for 10 minutes max. The alternate method of removal is to spray a cloth with alcohol and manually rub the lube off each case. When using this lube, the casefeeder plate needs to be cleaned more often since it gets sticky.[6e]

Why does this oily lube need to be removed? This lube causes cases to not momentarily adhere to the barrel chamber walls. This causes an increase in breechface thrust which accelerates wear of the bolt and locking lugs.[2n]

D–Other products. Over the years, I have occasionally used two non aerosol liquid water soluble pump sprays($10)– RCBS case slick and Frankford Arsenal. Apply lightly, wait a minute and then size the case. They do not leave a "sticky feel" and are useful for a quick lubrication.[24]

Some reloaders still like to use an old method–the lube pad. The RCBS pad is ideal because it is a foam pad that does not leave fibers like other types. Use the specific RCBS Case Lube-2 to prep the pad.[24/27]

These water soluble lubes are easily removed after loading by placing a batch on a damp towel and rolling them back and forth. This is the method suggested in many shooting forums.

For the rare individual case that needs to be lubricated,

use the Hornady unique case lube($5 for 4 oz. tub). This is a waterproof natural wax–dab your finger in the wax and apply to the case. It is ready to be sized without waiting.[24] Some reloaders like to lube the first 3–5 cases of a sizing session with this wax and then switch to DCL.

E–Case denting. Too much case lube and other factors can dent cases especially at the case shoulders. Experience will determine the correct amount of lube. Other factors include plugged vent holes and dirty sizing dies. Quality sizing dies have a vent hole in the die threads near the neck area. This hole vents trapped air–keep this hole open with a wire before a sizing session since dry lube will plug it up. Beware of nickel cases that tend to shed nickel plating and plug up the hole.[15a]

The other cause is dirty sizing dies. Before a sizing session take the sizing die apart. Clean the die and the neck mandrel to remove old and dried case lube–use a brush and solvent appropriate for the type of lube used. Polishing the expander mandrel on the decapping stem can also be part of the die preparations–these are very important preventive measures.[15a/2n]

11. Stuck cases.

A–Cause. Stuck cases are caused by inadequate lubrication, case separation or an unrecognized broken shellholder/shellplate.[2n]

Avoiding inadequate lubrication–my choice of rifle case lube is the lanolin based one from Dillon(DCL). In preparing the sizing die, I spray the lube in the sizing die to include the stem mandrel and allow it to dry. It is oily and it lubricates even the early rifle cases that enter the sizing die.[2n] IMHO, I have not stuck a long rifle case when using DCL.

With reloading experience you will learn that when the sizing ram-force is too great–stop, because you are about to stick a case. Pull out the case if it is not too late and relube the die and or relube the cases and the case mouths.[12e/15b]

Despite all of these preparations and preventive measures, when you get a stuck case you need a "stuck case remover kit".

B–How it works and products. Using a stuck case remover–take the sizing die out of press and place it in a vise with the case pointing up. The goal is to save the sizing die and throw away the case. The kits include drill bit, tap, allen screw/wrench and remover body. The steps are as follows:[24]

- Drill bottom of primer pocket out
- Apply the threading tap to the drill hole and turn clockwise
- Insert the "body" on top of case
- Insert the screw through the body into the tapped threads

- Turn the screw with allen wrench till the body lifts up and removes the stuck case–a simple process that saves the die

All major manufactures provide their own stuck case remover that fits on all dies. RCBS($19), Lyman($18), Redding($22),Hornady($16).[24]

The Dillon XL 650 has a unique situation that can lead to a stuck case–and it has happened to me with a pistol round. If the case insert slide spring is weak or broken, the slide will not push the case completely into the shellplate. This off side case can still allow the case to enter the sizing die but slip out of the shellplate and get stuck in the sizing die on the down stroke.[20] The stuck case is then removed using this method.

C–Dillon die method. A stuck case can be easily removed to save the die by using this method. The stuck case/die is left in the press. The retaining nut is released and the decapping pin is turned down until the case starts to be pushed out. After the case is loosened, remove the decapping stem/pin. Apply pliers to the case and gently tap the pliers with a hammer. The stuck case generally falls out. This process is well explained in the instruction manual enclosed with the rifle die. There is a video on you tube called "Removing stuck rifle case from Dillon full length sizing die" that clearly shows how this process is done correctly.

12. Gages(also spelled gauges)

A–Case length gages. There are two basic types. The simplest is the Lyman E-Zee($20) case length gage. An easy hand held aluminum plate that sorts cases quickly and accurately to determine if cases are over the maximum case length per industry standard. This tool is much quicker than calipers and works for over 70 popular pistol/rifle cases.[24]

The other style is the Lyman case gage($22). This is a one piece non adjustable steel cylinder. Drop the case in the cylinder–if it extends beyond the gage, it is longer than maximum length. Each gage is caliber specific. Like all case length gages, they should be used after sizing.[24]

B–Headspace (HS) gages. Clarification follows:[12f]

Headspace is the distance from the head of the cartridge to the face of the bolt.

Excessive headspace occurs when the distance between the head and bolt is too long. When firing the case, it has farther to travel before it hits the bolt. This situation can lead to higher pressures. Another result of excessive head-space is the failure to pop the primer since the firing pin cannot reach the primer.

Inadequate headspace is the situation where cases get too long and prevent the bolt from closing.[12f]

With this information, cases headspace according to their specific design, A list of common cartridges is as follows:[12f]

- Rimmed cartridges headspace on the rim
- Belted magnums headspace on the belt
- Bottle necked rimless headspace on the shoulder
- Straight walled rimless headspace on the case mouth–this includes auto pistol cases.[12f]

Headspace gages have become a popular item and the market has moved from the single to the multiple hole chambers. These gages are generally sized to the minimum side of the SAAMI specs. Here is a list of some popular ones:[6f]

- Dillon single caliber headspace gage for pistols($16)
- LE Wilson single caliber gage for pistol($18) and rifle($30)
- EGW–7($20). This is a 7 hole chamber made of aircraft aluminum. An economical item for volume cartridge testing The holes are bored with clymer reamers that are also used to ream barrel chambers. Like other similar gages, they measure minimum case diameter and maximum overall length. I recently used this gage to check 1000–9mm and it nicely picked out failures.
- EGW–50($100). Same as above but with 50 holes

- Shock Bottle($100) sold by Amazon. It is machined to normal SAAMI specs–not undersized. The 100 holes match Dillon/MTM ammo boxes so you can double flip checked rounds directly to ammo boxes–avoids repicking each checked round into the ammo boxes
- Hundo-100($100). Same as Shock Bottle above.[6f]

Note–keep in mind that lead cast bullets are .001 larger in diameter than jacketed bullets and can fit snug in headspace case gages.

I used a case gage on loaded 9mm and 38 special cowboy loads. By using a headspace case gage I found the following failures:

- Split cases is the most frequent finding. The cases can lead to the high pressures from a bullet setback or jam a lever action rifle used in cowboy action shooting
- Bulged cases along the entire body
- Belled cases that failed to crimp
- High primers. When the loaded cartridge is placed in the gage, I rub my finger on the primer to detect a high primer.
- Many other loading defects too numerous to mention.

C–Calipers. This is a universal case and cartridge testing tool. Used in conjunction with other gages, it is a necessary tool on the reloading bench. Dillon sells the two stainless steel types(not plastic)–dial($28) and electronic digital($40). These have a proven track record for longer life and have a satin chrome finish to minimize glare. The measuring faces are hardened, ground and capped. These calipers easily read up to .001 inch.[1a]

13. Case prep tools.

There are two reasons to need to perform case preparation–reaming out crimped primer pockets and cleaning trimmed case mouths. Most reloaders of volume ammo do not clean primer pockets–a technique common with benchrest shooters. As a practical volume reloader I only use manual tools for two reasons. The first, I only trim rare hunting rifle cases, and some pistol 44 magnum hot hunting loads that require a heavy crimp. The second, I discard any case that has a crimped primer pocket.

A–Basic/manual. A hand held basic tool is available from most major manufacturers. I have the Lyman brand($23). All these units have the similar features:[24]

- Compact hand held double ended tool
- Can chamfer the inside and outside of case mouth burrs

- Can clean large and small primer pockets
- Can remove primer pocket crimps
- Has a knurled aluminum handle
- One piece design allows storage of all four accessory heads.[24]

B–Powered centers. The reloader who generates large batches of trimmed cases generally uses a power trimmer or a powered case prep center. Here are three fairly economical types:[24]

1. Hornady Lock-N-Load case prep duo($45) and trio($95).[28]

- The Duo is a hand held powered trimmer that uses 8/32 threaded units and has two turning heads. It is powered by a lithium battery and comes with a charger
- The Trio is a table model that is electrically powered. It has three turning heads and also uses 8/32 threaded tips
- Both come with chamfering/deburring heads
- Optional primer pocket crimp reamer($9) and pocket cleaner($5).[24/28]

2. RCBS Trim Mate case prep center($120).[24/27]

- This is a 110 volt five gear driven heads

- It includes: chamfering head, deburring head, small and large primer pocket and neck brushes
- Optional–primer pocket crimp remover and flash hole deburring tool(both for $28).[24/27]

3. Lyman X-Press case prep center($135). This is an all inclusive system providing all the necessary accessories as follows:[24]

- Chamfering and deburring tools
- S and L primer pocket uniformer and crimp reamer
- Four case neck brushes–20-30-38-45 calibers
- Mica case neck lube
- Removable brass shaving pan with clean up brush.[24]

14. Swaging tools. These are specific tools to remove the primer pockets of military brass, some commercial rifle brass and some commercial pistol brass.

A–Manual/powered. Already mentioned in section13 above. Another simple method involves inserting a crimp reaming tip in a drill press and set it to proper depth.[11c]

B–Single stage press. An example is the CH4D swager($35). It includes:

- Fits in any press
- It removes small and large primer pocket crimps
- The swage punches are hardened steel

- Available through CH4D.com/products/equipment

C–Super swager. The Dillon Super Swage 600($104). This unit is for large batch jobs. It bolts to the bench for stability. With this mechanism, the case is supported from the inside and holds the rims in place so they cannot be torn off. A hardened swage rod(S and L) simply rolls the crimp away–not reaming. It will handle all calibers except 9mm but there is an adapter for this caliber($15). A compound cam lever assures ease of operation and a perfect alignment of each round.[1a]

15. Shellholders. This section is included to point out that individual shellholders are available through RCBS for $8 each. There are kits such as Lyman shellholder pack of twelve($39) that will fit 75 calibers. Another is the kit from Hornady–a pack of five($17) that will also fit several calibers. If you use a single stage, turret or some progressive presses, you will need shellholders.[24] If your progressive press has caliber specific shellplates, you do not need shellholders.

16. Primer tube stands. The reloaders that pre load their primer tubes do benefit from these aftermarket holders. One of these($20) is from uniquetek.com/product/T1567. It holds 12 primer tubes–made of U shaped plates and three rods to make a stable free standing stand. Another is from inlinefabrication.com/collections/press-accessories. A simple 4 slot rack that also holds 12 tubes but mounts on the wall, shelf or bench.

In this chapter's summary, I hoped to give you different choices for each of the ten necessary items. In addition, the other optional items depends on your personal needs and habits. Unfortunately the costs incurred are for these necessary tools of the trade.

CHAPTER-6

RELOADING DIES

Introduction.

1. Full length sizing.

    A–Full length/RCBS
    B–RCBS small base and X–die
    C–Dillon pistol dies
    D–Dillon carbide rifle dies
    E–Wasp-waist
    F–Result of repeated sizing

2. Other sizing methods.

    A–Neck sizing
    B–Partial sizing

3. Belling dies.

    A–Degrees of belling
    B–Standard dies with M die
    C–Boat tail jacketed bullets
    D–Dillon expander funnel
    E–Bullet feeder funnel

4. Dillon powder die/measure.

    A–Powder types

    B–Powder not falling

    C–Discolored powder

    D–Brass sticking to powder tube

    E–Powder spillage

    F–Checking powder charges

5. Crimping dies.

    A–Roll crimp

    B–Taper crimp

    C–Factory crimp

6. Dies for unique situations.

    A–Cowboy dies

    B–Match grade dies

    C–Special feature dies

        –G-RX dies

        –U dies

        –Floating die toolhead

        –Toolhead clamping kit

7. Comparing brand of dies.

Introduction.

Sizing is the most challenging and yet the very important first step in the reloading process. We do sizing to industry standards to assure cartridges will fit in any gun of the same caliber.[13c] Modern dies for practical volume reloading are generally produced by the"big five"–Lee, Hornady, Lyman, RCBS and Dillon. These dies can produce excellent ammo for plinking, target, competition and hunting loads. For bench-rest and long range shooters, one usually uses high precision dies from Forster, Redding and Sinclair–not part of this book. Many of the "big five" also provide special competition and or match grade variations of their basic dies–these will be included in this chapter with standard dies.

Sizing involves several extra "prep" steps to assure proper results. These include:

- Case cleaning and polishing
- Selecting cases especially with range brass
- Case inspection to rule out defects–especially split cases and crimped primer pockets
- Case lubing for 44 magnum, 45 colt and rifle cases
- Dismantle sizing die for cleaning and lubricating
- Special attention to check for proper case placement in shell-holder/shellplate

1. Full length sizing.

A–Full length/RCBS. Full length sizing occurs when the die touches the shellholder/shellplate–this will actually bump the case shoulder. A nice feature of single stage and turret presses is that the press handle can cam-over with some mild resistance–guaranteeing absolute full length sizing.[88]

I use Dillon pistol dies and RCBS rifle dies. The RCBS standard two die set includes a full length sizing and a combination seat/crimp die. The sizing die has a decapping pin and a neck expander on the decapping stem. Vent holes along the threads prevent case damage. This includes dimples and dents along the neck or shoulder, caused by trapped air or excess case lubricant.[24/27]

B–RCBS small base and X Die. The small base die sizes the case body somewhat smaller and sets the shoulder back more than standard dies. This will insure proper cartridge functioning in semi-automatic, pumps and lever action rifles. Use of this die is NOT recommended for bolt action rifles.[27]

The X Die eliminates the need for repeated case trimming. Starting with equally trimmed cases, a special mandrel contacts the case mouth and reduces the neck growth rate. It is likely that another trimming will not be necessary during the life of the case.[27]

C–Dillon pistol dies. These are three die sets with a full length carbide sizing die. This decapping/sizing die has a spring on the top of the stem that compresses on the ram upstroke an releases with a snap at the end of the stroke to kick the spent primer off the tip of the decapping pin. This prevents the primer from sticking to the decapping pin and pulling the primer back in the pocket–a condition that can cause a complication in station two(detonation-more in chapter 13).[6g]

D–Dillon carbide rifle dies. Dillon offers rifle dies only in a few calibers–223, 300 AAC Blackout, 308, 30-06. The three die sets are available as standard sets or sets with a carbide sizing die. The carbide sizing die decreases the amount of needed case lubrication, although a small amount of case lube is still needed. The major "carbide" advantage is in die longevity. The longevity of a standard rifle sizing die is +- 40,000 cases whereas the carbide die is +- 750,000 cases. Also the carbide sizing die has significant scratch resistance from dirty cases. Even with minimal case lube, there is very little chance of sticking a case in a carbide rifle die.[9b]

The cost for carbide rifle sizing dies is high. The Dillon Blue Press lists the three die set with a carbide sizing die for 223 & 308 at $170 and the 30-06 at $275.[1a] Carbide rifle sizing dies are also available through RCBS, Lyman and Hornady.

According to multiple forums, the 30-30 case does not need a carbide sizing die. It is one of the easier rifle cases to size because the case is slightly tapered from the base to the shoulder. This taper allows a fully seated case in the sizing die to back off just enough to freely come out of the die.

E–Wasp waist. Sizing in auto pistol cases(9mm,40S&W and 45acp) causes a unique loaded appearance. These cases have a slight taper from base to case mouth which causes a bullet to be a "tight press fit"–a slight ridge in the case where the bullet ends. This produces the appearance of the "wasp waist". Lead bullet diameters are .001" larger than jacketed bullets and so have a greater "wasp waist" appearance than jacketed bullets. This loaded appearance is good in preventing bullet setback. The other factor that increases the: "wasp waist" appearance is cases that have thicker metal such as S&B and CBC cases.[8a/9c]

F–Result of repeated sizing. When a cartridge is fired, the case brass expands and then springs back. With repeated expansion and contraction, the brass "work hardens" and loses its elasticity to contract after firing. This leads to rounds failing to chamber, sticking in sizing dies or begin to have split mouths. For these reasons, most cases reload 6-8 times before these problems begin to occur–worse in rifles.[12h]

2. Other sizing methods. A very popular method is the one that makes ammo only fit a specific gun. The ammo is made so tightly to that gun's chamber that accuracy is improved. It requires a fired cartridge from the specific gun that is sized only to the point that the shoulder is pushed back a

few thousandths of an inch and the neck is sized to industry standards by the following two methods–neck and partial sizing.[12i] Although this method belongs more to benchrest and long range competition shooters, I include it in this book because of hunters who shoot at 300-500 yards and benefit from better accuracy.

A–Neck sizing. Neck sizing is achieved by using neck sizing bushings that do not stretch case necks. The ID of the case neck should be .003-.005" smaller than the bullet diameter– this will give a good fit. To achieve this critical tension, you need to use the specific bushing for your bullet. Redding neck sizing bushings are available in .001" increments for most calibers. Steel bushings are $16 each and the titanium are $27each.[12j/24]

> FYI–To determine proper bushing size, measure the outside neck diameter of a loaded cartridge. Then subtract .001-.002". to allow for brass spring back and bullet tension. For more detailed information go to accurateshooter.com.[12j]

With repeated neck sizing, the cartridge will eventually not fit in the chamber from repeated fire forming. You will then need to full length size the case and restart your neck sizing over.[12j]

B–Partial sizing. Partial sizing is done with regular full

length sizing dies. The goal is to only push back the shoulder by .002". To achieve this you need to use very specific gages for this precise result. RCBS makes a "Precision Mic" for each caliber($45) that measures the sizing effect on the shoulder–it measures from the datum point on the case shoulder to the base of the case.[24/27]

What is the accuracy difference using these sizing methods? Factory ammo will give you a 1-2 MOA. Full length sizing can give you sub MOA. Neck/partial sizing will even give you more accuracy. It seems that the difference between full length and partial/neck sizing accuracy is based on differences in pressures that produce variations in speed.[12j]

In my experience the woods hunter shooting 100 yards will use factory ammo. The 200+ yard hunter will use full length sizing. The 300-500 yard hunter will rely on partial/ neck sizing. The benchrest and extreme range rifle shooter will use the many extra techniques that are beyond this book.

3. Belling dies.

A–Degree of belling. You only need enough bell for the case to accept and hold a bullet long enough to enter the seating die–even if you have to hold a bullet with your fingers to help guide it into the seating die. You are over belling if the bullet falls in the case. If you need to quantify the amount of belling, measure a sized case mouth and the belled case mouth should be .01 to .02". larger. Try the .01" flare first since the least belling saves on neck splits.[9d]

B–Standard dies with M-die. If you are using a standard 2-die rifle set to load lead or flat base jacketed bullets, you will need a belling die. This pertains to any press that does not use the powder funnel to expand the case mouth. Lyman produces a quality belling die called the M-die. This die works in two steps. The first step expands the inside of the case neck to just under bullet diameter. The second step expands the case mouth to slightly over bullet diameter.[24]

C–Bevel base "boat tails". This base modification allows you to use jacketed bullets in standard 2-die sets without an M-die. For my hunting bullets, I use Hornady Interlock SST bullets which are boat tails.

D–Dillon expander funnel. If you use the Dillon XL 650 you do need a belling die for jacketed(excluding boattails) bullets. For lead, coated or plated bullets in pistols, the degree of belling desired can be achieved by moving the powder die upward/downward in the toolhead.[9e]

E–Bullet feeder belling. Any standard belling die including the M-die and Dillon funnel is not to be used in any bullet feeder. Each of the commercial bullet feeders has their own belling dies that allows holding a proper bullet orientation and solid entry into the case mouth.[9e]

4. Dillon powder die/measure.

This powder die/measure combo at station 2 is crucial in delivering a reproducible powder charge. Quality ammo requires a uniform charge weight. This delivery system is the same in all of Dillon pistol/rifle presses including the Square Deal B.

A–Powder types. Dillon charge weight accuracy is based on the type of powder used. Ball or spherical is best. Initially the variability is +- 0.1gr. As the powder settles in the hopper's baffle, variability improves. Flake powder has greater variability–as much as +- 0.2gr.

Be cautious to use flake powder at maximum charge because of the high variability. Tubular powder is the worse. The variability is as high as 0.5gr. but when you are loading some 50 grains in a rifle case–the variation of 0.5gr. is of little significance.[11e]

B–Powder not falling. Irrelevant of the type of powder used, there are some common causes for this problem:[11g]

- Extruded tubular powder tends to "log jam" in the funnel–so decrease your speed on upstroke to allow enough time for the powder to drop. Another method, give a mild tap to the powder mechanism to guarantee that all the powder is out
- Use the powder bar size appropriate for the charge weight.

- Make sure you bell enough to move the powder bar all the way over. Verify there is enough tension on the failsafe wing nut to fully retract the powder bar
- Keep 2/3 of hopper full
- Keep the interior of powder funnel and drop tube clean by using an alcohol soaked cotton swab. Occasionally the powder funnel needs polishing
- Powder measure parts need changing when worn out.[11g]

C–Discolored powder. If powder is left in the hopper for extended periods, it will eventually turn green. The powder reacts with the plastic hopper and it also turns the plastic green. This color change is a sign that the powder has degraded and will also start to clump. This powder should be discarded. As a good practice, return powder to the original container if you are not planning to reload within 24 hours.[9h]

D–Brass sticking to drop tube. This problem is prevalent in new brass. This brass does not have the carbon residue in the case necks which acts as a lubricant. These are other examples:[4n]

- Using a rotary tumbler with liquid cleaning agent can clear the case necks of this carbon lubricant
- Static electricity. Wipe the tube and funnel with a laundry anti-cling strip
- Polish the funnel

- Tumble new brass before use
- Spray "one shot" or similar case lube on the powder funnel and inside the drop tube–this does not affect the powder. Let the lube thoroughly dry before use
- Too much belling can lead to sticky brass.[4n]

E–Powder spillage. Large charge loads close to the top is a real problem with straight wall cases. If you are going too fast in the arm upstroke, powder will flip out when the shellplate stops rotating with a snap.[9i] It helps to slow down and wait for the powder to drop completely into the case. This is especially true of short cases such as 9mm–plus some case lengths are shorter per different manufacturers.[9j]

Another solution is to use a powder that uses a smaller volume to achieve the desired velocity such as Titegroup. IMHO the ultimate solution to this problem is the installation of the HIT Factor Bearing Kit mentioned in Chapter 4.
F–Checking powder charges. The issue is how often do you really need to check powder charges when using a Dillon powder measure.

These are useful guidelines:[6h]

- The first ten charges will vary until the powder settles under the baffle. Tapping the powder mechanism will shorten this process. Some reloaders discard the first half dozen charges

- Keep the hopper at least 50% full or greater
- After the powder settles and you have little charge variability, check the charge every 100 rounds when it is time to add primers
- Keep the same speed and cadence. Most Dillon powder measures will throw a heavier charge if you stop reloading for more than a few minutes. This is good advice if you are loading at maximum pressures
- Don't be a "type A" and check powder charges every ten rounds. You will be chasing a .1gr. normal variability and end up with very unequal charges.[6h]

5. Crimping. We crimp our handloads to avoid the bullet from falling out of the case or from being pushed back in the case(bullet setback). This is especially important with rifles that have a loading tube, heavy recoil in revolvers and chambering in auto pistols.

A–Roll crimp. This is the most used method in practical reloading. It involves turning the case mouth into a bullet crimp groove or cannelure–that headspaces on the pistol/rifle rim, belt of mag cartridges and shoulder of standard rifle. This is true only if the cartridges are all in the min-max length range. Over and under crimping are the result of case length variations beyond the min-max case length.[12k]

B–Taper crimp. When the bullet is tightly pushed into the case body, it prevents the bullet from moving in or out. In this situation, the case mouth edge must remain prominent since it is the mouth edge that headspaces the round. This crimping method is the standard in auto pistol(9mm, 40S&W and 45 acp) as well as in automatic rifles.[12k]

The goal in taper crimping is to completely remove the belling without turning the case mouth into the bullet. Over crimping will cause the cartridge to fail headspacing on the case mouth or start bulging the case body or shoulder. Using case lube will ease taper crimping but if your cases are getting old, you may still start experiencing this "bulging" even if you are not over crimping.[12k]

Roll and taper crimping can be accomplished by either a 2-die or a 3-die set. The 2-die set allows seating and crimping in the same step. The 3-die set provides a separate seating and crimping die. The arguments as to which set is best will continue for years–sometimes your press toolhead limits which set can be used.[12k]

C–Factory crimp. Lee produces a crimping die that mimics the "factory ammo crimp" and comes in two types–pistol and rifle.

The Lee rifle factory crimp features a collet that squeezes the case mouth longitudinally in four locations–into the crimp groove or cannelure. This mechanism makes it impossible to buckle the case from excessive roll or taper crimping. Case length is not so crucial with this collet system as long as COAL is within min-max length. It provides a firm crimp that will not allow bullet setback in tubular magazines–I use this crimp in my 30-30 hot hunting loads and never had a bullet setback. According to Lee, this factory crimp die provides a uniform pressure curve which leads to better accuracy.[12L]

The pistol Lee factory crimp comes in two types. One is for revolver cartridges and mimics a roll crimp. The other is for auto cartridges and mimics a taper crimp.[12L]

6. Dies for unique situations.

Beyond the standard reloading dies presented, there are dies that can be used to solve problems.

A–Cowboy dies. These are premium carbide dies built to slightly different dimensions to allow optimum loading of lead bullets.[24]

Each manufacturer seems to provide their own unique features. An example is Hornady's Cowboy dies–their seater die features: an adjustment screw, a built in crimper, a locking retainer spring and a floating bullet alignment sleeve. This last feature pre aligns the bullet and case before seating.[17c]

The Dillon carbide pistol dies provides the ease of cleaning for the sizing and seating dies. By releasing the clamp, the inserts fall out for ease of cleaning and reinserting to maintain zero settings. The previously mentioned wide radius of the sizing die allows case ease in entering the sizing die and the spring loaded decapping pin prevents primers from reentering the primer pocket. Like all 3-die sets, it provides a separate crimping die.[1a]

B–Match grade dies. These are finely crafted dies for ultimate accuracy demanded by serious shooters–especially hunters shooting 300-500 yards. RCBS has a Gold Medal Match 2-die set($115). It features a full length sizing die that uses precision machined neck sizing bushings(sold separately) to size the case neck just enough to provide the exact amount of bullet tension without over working the case–this is the same info provided in 2–A above. The seater die features a micrometer adjustment knob so that the bullet depth can be precisely set. The micrometer is connected to a free floating self centering bullet seating system.[24/27]

C–Special feature dies.

G-RX die. The Redding carbide base sizing die kit($82). Some autoloaders can produce a bulge at the bottom of the case which standard sizing dies cannot reach. This is a push through die–simply push the case through the die and the bulge is removed. The push rod is in the press and fits the case being rid of the bulge. Then resize/decap using your standard dies.[24]

This base "bulge" can cause a cartridge to not fully enter the chamber–the striker may fall and fire the round out of battery. This may be a dangerous event. However if you case gage your ammo, it will pick out these defective cartridges.[6i]

U-die. Evolution Gun Works makes an undersize die($30). If you use range brass shot by some Glocks and others, the cases may need to be undersized to fit in your gun.[38] This undersized die is .001" smaller in diameter than standard sizing dies. The bottom edge of the die is radiused which sizes the case further down. This die is useful in pistols that have unusually tight chambers or in cases bulged near the base.[5c]

Floating die toolheads. Uniquetek.com/product/T1387 sells the Whidden Gunworks toolhead($80) which has lock rings that allow the sizing and seating dies to float. This allows the dies to center over each cartridge–for the best possible alignment and more concentric ammunition.[26d]

Toolhead clamping kit. uniquetek.com/products/T1230 sells the Whidden clamped toolhead($37) kit. It enables the toolhead to be clamped to the XL 650 press frame. To achieve this, place dummy rounds in each position and run the platform up into the dies–followed by final tightening of the screws. It stabilizes the die to the shellplate alignment, improves crimp repeatability and improves bullet concentricity.[9k]

7. Comparing brand of dies.

Given reasonably good dies and quality components, a skilled volume reloader can usually produce quality ammo.

Any "ranking" of dies is IMHO likely based on personal preferences–this is a list of some engineering differences that may influence your individual needs:[68/69]

- Major manufacturers provide dies in 2 or 3-die sets
- Lee offers their "factory crimp die" as an alternative to roll/taper crimping. According to Lee, separate crimping with a 3-die set or Lee factory crimp has the advantage of not shaving lead, coating or plating during seating
- If you don't use a Dillon press, you will need a Lyman M-die to expand the case mouth for lead, coated, plated and non boat tail jacketed bullets
- Hornady includes a nice sleeve to aid in alignment of the bullet prior to seating
- RCBS sizing dies has vent holes in the threads that prevent dents in the case neck and shoulder. Their X die nearly eliminates repeated case trimming
- Redding makes precision dies for accurate rifle ammo.[68/69]
- In comparing prices for pistol carbide dies: Lee $30, RCBS $45, Hornady $45, Dillon $67 and Redding $93.[34]

IMHO–for my needs as a volume practical reloader, Dillon pistol dies are my choice for my Dillon XL 650. My rifle dies are RCBS 2-die sets.

In closing this chapter on reloading dies, it is time to check your product. After loading +- six rounds, stop and verify that these rounds are usable. For pistols, place all six rounds in a cartridge case gage as a first quality check. The next step is to verify that the pistol rounds enter the revolver cylinder properly or chamber in the auto pistol barrel with a good "plunk test". For rifle rounds, place each in a cartridge case gage–assuming they pass then safely place the rounds in the rifle chambers to verify a proper fit and extraction. It is always wise to test fire a few rounds before loading a full batch of ammo.[13c]

These basic steps will not only assure good ammo, but may avoid a terrible frustrating reloading outcome–a batch of bad ammo that needs to be dismantled!

CHAPTER-7

PRIMERS

Introduction

1. Anatomy of a primer.

2. Primer types.

    A–Large pistol primers
    B–Small pistol/small rifle primers
    C–Large pistol magnum primers
    D–45 acp primers
    E–Rifle primers

3. Priming adjustments/seating depth.

4. Failure to feed.

5. Dillon RF-100.

    A–Adjustable rheostat
    B–Feed adapter plate
    C–Base spring adjustment/noise reduction
    D–Flipped primers
    E–Volume filling

6. My experience with primers.

Introduction

A chapter on primers may initially seem boring, of questionable significance or of low practical usefulness to the volume reloader. The old saying "a primer is a primer" followed with "there is no practical difference between any of the commercial primers", will be dismissed.

At the end of this chapter, you should be able to apply the following acquired facts into a usable framework for volume reloading. The other portion of this chapter will cover how primers can properly function in your press and in the RF-100 primer loader.

1. Anatomy of a primer. There is nothing magical about primers. You can visualize and understand how they work. A primer is made up of a steel cup with priming compound in its base. The compound is covered by an anvil that has three legs. These legs need to rest on the base of the primer pocket. Upon firing the anvil will crush the priming compound as long as the anvil legs are touching the primer pocket base.[12m]

To help understand this information, lets deal with a high primer—a cause of misfire in auto pistols. A high primer requires too much of the firing pin energy to fully seat the primer and apply the anvil legs to the primer pocket base. The result is that the primer shows a minor firing pin dent and a misfire–fire it again and it will go off since the anvil legs have now properly seated on the first strike.[12m]

2. Primer characteristics.

A–Large pistol primers. The difference between standard and magnum primers is a velocity variance of +-40 fps. This varies with different powders and guns. This difference is important when you are loading a standard primer with a maximum load–the change in pressure and velocity with a magnum primer may be a serious issue.[6k]

B–Small pistol-small rifle primers. If you are not loading to max, the small magnum pistol and small rifle primers are generally felt to be interchangeable with standard small pistol primers. They are however harder and so some pistols(especially striker fired) may cause light strikes or misfires.[15c/8b] My NRV will fire both standard and magnum small pistol primers with a reduced hammer spring of 14 lbs. I do not interchange with small rifle primers.

C–Large pistol magnum primers. The choice of standard vs. magnum primers in large pistol calibers depends on the type of powder used. If you use a fast burning powder like Titegroup, the standard primer is very adequate. When using a slow burning powder like 2400 or H-110, you need a magnum primer for proper ignition.[8c]

D–45 acp primers. 45 acp cases are available with either

small or large pistol primer pockets. Although the large pistol type is mostly used, it is wise to understand the problems using the alternate type that is often found in range pick or lost brass matches. When loading with SPP you have a lower velocity than with a LPP–the solution is to increase the charge by 0.1-0.2 gr. with SPP. The alternative is to use SRP or SMPP. Whatever primer you choose, you need to check your choice on a chronograph since you are only trying to maintain the velocity produced by the large pistol primers.[8d/8e]

E–Rifle primers. Rifle primers are harder than pistol primers and the firing pin blow is also stronger to accommodate the tougher cup. They also contain more priming compound to match the large volume of powder in rifle cartridges.[70]

Magnum primers are hotter than standard primers and are usually used with ball powder which is harder to ignite than flake or extruded powders. They are also used in magnum or other large capacity cases. It is often recommended to use magnum primers when the cartridges are to be used in less than 20 degrees F.[70]

It is the opinion of many reloaders that Winchester primers are the hottest, Federal/CCI are the middle brands and Remington the mildest. There are so many pressure/velocity variations in all types of large rifle primers, that it is strongly recommended to use a reloading manual. This reference will guide you to the proper brand and type of primer to use.[70]

IMHO, whenever you are loading at max velocity and

are planning to interchange primers, you should check your velocity on a chronograph. It is not only a matter of excessive pressures/velocities, it is also a matter of making the "power factor" you need in your sport.[8e]

3. Priming adjustments/seating depth. There are no adjustments for primer seating depths on the Dillon XL 650. The priming system has a "hard stop" while seating that will seat primers at least .001" below flush–it can be deeper depending on different headstamps. This "hard stop" is superior to the hand held priming tools that rely on feeling the primer seat. Beyond this "hard stop" there are factors that will affect primer's final depth:[1g]

- A tight shellplate bolt is required to prevent the shellplate lifting off the priming punch
- Anvil height of various primer brands
- Variations in primer pocket depths by case brand
- Some primer brands have harder steel and are harder to seat. IMHO–Federals are softer and easiest to seat compared to Winchesters which are harder and more difficult to seat
- All brands of primers can flip or go sideways in station 2 if the priming punch assembly is loose.[1g]

Note: If you wish to confirm that your primers are at least .001" below flush, place a straight edge across the head–if you see light between the primer and the straight edge, it is below flush. For the reloader who needs to know the exact measurement below flush, you need to use a depth micrometer.[5d]

4. Failure to feed. There are general and some unique situations that will cause a failure to feed primers in the Dillon XL 650– these are presented with some solutions:[11f]

- The basics–take the priming system apart, clean, lubricate and check for broken parts especially springs
- Primers sticking in dirty pickup tubes, RF-100 filler tube and priming system magazine tube. Clean the tubes of priming compound residue by pushing the end of a Q-tip swab soaked in alcohol. Use a 22 cleaning rod with large primer tubes and the black plastic rod for small primer tubes
- Add a 45 long colt case on top of the black plastic push rod to add weight and help in pushing primers down in the magazine tube
- When primers are getting stuck in any type of tube, check for a bad batch of primers that are out of round(concentricity) or have a long anvil leg sticking out of primer cup. A bad batch needs to be discarded

- The primer indexing arm spring is weak, broken or crunched and the arm cannot reach the next hole to index the primers.[11f]
- A common cause–defective low primer alarm. The buzzer does not sound off and so you run out of primers with a fully loaded shellplate. The simple solution is to add more primers and cycle the primer indexing arm with your finger till the primers come around. Then replace the alarm battery, fix the problem or replace the low primer alarm.[5d]

NOTE–How to manage a stuck primer in any of the primer tubes.

Push downward on the anvil side to maintain the normal directional flow—pushing on the shiny cup side will likely scratch the tube or could fire the primer. With small primer tubes you push with the black plastic push rod and with large primer tubes you can push with a 22 cal. cleaning rod. Gently push with mild to moderate continuous pressure—never tap, slam or use a hammer. Some reloaders spray WD-40 down the tube before pushing and then clean the WD-40 off with an alcohol swab. Containing the tube in a ½ inch steel pipe to do the maneuver is very wise. Always point the tube ends away from you.[6j] Note: primers that soaked in WD-40 need to be discarded.

If the stuck primers come out easily, there are likely no further consequences. If it comes out hard, the tube has likely been scratched and may be a problem in the future. Do this procedure reasonably and safely, if it fails then Dillon will likely replace the tube. After all these years of reloading, I finally had a stuck primer in the RF-100 filler tube. Dillon replaced the tube and housing at no charge–the agent's comment was to thank me for not pushing this primer beyond reasonable pressure.

5. Dillon RF-100.

This is a great automatic primer filler that eliminates the task of manually filling pickup tubes. Thanks to Dillon, you simply pour 100 primers from their box into the top platform and press the start button. The machine will load the primers into the filler tube in +- 2 minutes. The cost is $335 for one size primer and an extra $49 for the other size primer.[87]

The platform is the workhorse of this machine and includes:[2r/91]

- It has a clear polycarbonate shield for protection and the unit should be operated with it on. It also reduces operational noise
- It should be kept clean of priming compound dust which can be explosive–clean it with alcohol

- It has a sweeper at 12 o'clock for double stacked primers. It has drop notches at 3 o'clock and near the plastic plate. These notches allow primers to fall off the ramp when they are upside down–the anvil side is not flat which makes these primers fall off
- It has a bead blast finish that keeps primers moving in the correct direction and gives the primers the traction from sliding back as they move up the ramp. A worn off surface necessitates a platform replacement.[2r/9l]

This machine can be an epic reloading tool or a heavy paper weight. It all depends on the proper tuning by the operator–if done right it will be the smoothest, trouble free, efficient and appreciated tool on your reloading bench.[2q] Here are some important tuning tips:

A–Adjustable rheostat. If you are buying a current model, it is included. If you have an older model, adding this unit is the most important upgrade you can get for +-$40. Many older machines that were abandoned can now be brought back with this rheostat. The adjustable dial varies the motor speed from slow to fast. The faster you run the motor the more the primers jump, fall off the ramp or flip.[9l]

Adjust the unit by starting slow and increase the speed to get the best smooth feeding action. The small primer adjustment may vary between brands and will certainly need readjustment when switching to large primers.[9l]

B–Feed adapter/plate. The feed adapter(red or blue) transfers primers from the platform ramp to the filler tube–it must JIGGLE. The screw under the feed adapter must be loosened 3/4 of a turn from a tight position. This allows the necessary jiggling for primers to enter the adapter.[2r]

The clear plastic plate on top of the ramp needs to be just snug enough to allow primers to enter but also force upside down primers to fall off the railing before entering the final ramp. Be patient to set this very important adjustment.[2r]

After a recent phone consultation with Dillon, Plate A is now used for small and large pistol primers as well as large rifle–the height of small pistol primers is +- .114", large pistol is +- .118" and large rifle is +-.124". Plate B is for higher primers such as large rifle magnum primers.

The A plate bottom has a ramp 3/4 of an inch before the primer falls in the filler tube–this is to tighten the space so the primers don't flip. Depending on the height, some primers are worse than others for flipping. It is up to you to determine which brand of primers works best in your RF-100. If the ramp is wearing off and is no longer thick enough for the brand of primer used, add a thin layer of "super glue" to increase the thickness of the ramp or best of all, replace the plate. The opposite occurs when using an unusual brand of taller primers that get stuck under the ramp–add a piece primer box cardboard under the plate to elevate the ramp off the primers. Never remove the plate and grind the ramp off because it ruins it from future use with regular primers.[2r]

C–Base spring adjustment/noise reduction. This maneuver is best seen on YouTube "Fine tuning the Dillon RF-100 to reduce noise, primers flipping and jumping". The black round base that holds the filler tube has an internal spring that needs to be modified. Once the spring is removed per video instruction, use both hands and turn the spring ends at least 3 near full turns simultaneously. This shortens the spring and will stiffen the middle portion of the spring but keep the ends soft and springy. The result is a much quieter and smoother action that keeps primers staying in proper position.[89]

D–Flipped primers. Flipping primers before entering the filler tube is undoubtedly the most irritating event using a Dillon RF-100. The above mentioned methods and fine tuning are crucial in controlling this problem. When all fails, try tilting the unit forward a bit and quickly go to a plate replacement.[9m] IMHO–CCI primers are "flippers" but less so with Winchester and not so with Federal.

E–Volume filling. Some reloaders use this filling tool while they are reloading and fill one tube at a time. This requires the machine to operate without your eyes watching. If a jam occurs while you are reloading, it stops your loading process and it becomes an irritation. The alternative method is to dedicate a time to load multiple tubes. By transferring the primers from the filler tube to pickup tubes(with the pickup tips capped with tape), you can prepare the exact number of tubes for your next planned reloading session. As previously mentioned, there are aftermarket racks that hold multiple tubes.

Adding primers to pickup tubes is a mindless job that is probably the only unpleasant event in reloading. I love my RF-100 because I have taken the time to fine tune it and it works like a charm. If you find the price a deterrent, then consider the Frankford Arsenal hand held Vibra-Prime for $50. The unique battery motorized agitation vibrates the primers in a primer tray and works them into the primer tubes. It comes with one universal primer tray, one small and large primer tube, and two universal tube adapters. It does require the user to be the operator but you can fill a pickup tube in a fraction of the time compared to picking primers from a flip tray.[24]

6. My experience with primers.

IMHO–Federal primers(small and large) are my favorite standard pistol primers. They are the easiest to prime, softest to fire off with light springs but require more attention when there is a resistance to priming–as with crimped primer pockets. CCI are the hardest and Winchester are more midland. Winchester is my second choice but since they go in harder than Federal, it is easier to get a high primer if not maintaining a uniform priming force. Yet I have been recently loading CCI primers since they are plentiful on the gun shop shelves. I have had a few problems with flipping primers in the RF-100 and a few getting stuck in the filler tube–but easily pushed out. Yet these are rare events and I do not hesitate to pick up CCI primers when others are not available. Yes, availability of primers has become the decision maker these days–if it becomes necessary I will try Wolfe primers.

I use magnum pistol primers in two situations. The first is in hot magnum hunting loads with slower burning pistol powders. The second is in Cowboy Shooting where we use such low powder charges that the magnum primer assures proper ignition.

My favorite large rifle primer is Winchester because it is the hottest–this is important to me since I load rifle hunting loads near max with its inherent large volume of powder. Yet I have used CCI and Federals without problems. I do not load magnum calibers and so I do not use magnum large rifle primers.

CHAPTER – 8

RELOADING 9MM

Introduction

1. Cartridge dimensions.

   A–COAL
   B–Go-No-Go gauges

2. Taper crimp.

3. Power Factor.

4. Sticking cases.

5. Primer types.

6. Other components.

   A–Powders
   B–Bullets

7. Flyers.

8. FAQ's.

   A–Case feeder jams

B–Ammo will not chamber

C–Case variations

D–Bullet seating crooked

E–Low velocity issues

F–9mm brass variations

G–Significance of seating depth variations

9. My 9mm reloading experience

A–Cases

B–Press modifications

C–Components

D–Stage by stage points of interest

E–Cartridge gage rejects

Introduction

The 9mm caliber goes by the name 9mm Luger, 9mm parabellum or 9X19 mm and is likely the most popular pistol caliber in the US. Visit any range to notice that most of the spent cases on the ground or floor are 9mm. The cases are more economical than other pistol cases and the supply is very good which helps to keep prices down. The low weight of its bullets also provides the best prices whether you use lead, plated, coated or jacketed bullets.

Reloading is usually done with a progressive press since shooting any auto pistol just seems to eat up a lot of ammo.

Reloading the 9mm provides its own set of issues which deserve the special attention found in this chapter.

1. Cartridge dimensions.

A–COAL. The 9mm maximum COAL is 1.169" so a loaded round will fit in the magazine. This is true of lead RN, jacketed HP and FMJ. The lead TC and SWC are usually shorter than 1.169".

Hornady's 9th edition manual shows a cartridge OAL of 1.050"–1.169". The case length is a minimum of .744" and a maximum of .754". The case mouth diameter post sizing is .380" whereas the post taper crimping diameter is .378"– .379". The load industry maximum pressure is 35,000 psi.[14a]

B–GO-NO-GO gage. The GO-NO-GO gage is my choice of nomenclature for a tool with so many different names. Often called headspace gage, cartridge gage, case gage, high primer gage and case neck split gage. It is called "GO" when it passes a case and "NO_GO" when it rejects a case. With a loaded round in the gage, the head must be flush with the top of the gage to pass. If the head is above or below the gage top, it fails and is a reject.

IMHO, these are some examples of "high rejects":

- Residual case mouth belling from inadequate crimping
- Excessive taper crimping that is bulging the case body

- Significant case mouth splits that can affect the grip tension
- Excessively long cases above maximum case length
- Base bulging from inadequate sizing

My examples of "low rejects":

- Excessive taper crimping without body bulging can remove the case mouth edge that is needed for head spacing
- Extremely short cases below minimum
- Wrong caliber such as the 380 auto

Testing for a high primer is part of using this gage. When the cartridge is in the gage, pass your finger over the primer and you will easily confirm whether the primer is high or properly seated. If a loaded round passes a GO-NO-GO gage, you can feel reassured that this round will pass the "plunk test" in your modern barrel chamber.

The GO-NO-GO gage is not forgiving and has tight SAAMI dimensions. The chamber of your pistol may have larger dimensions and may allow a gage reject to function properly in your pistol–it all depends on the size of your barrel chamber. Firing these gage rejects can be dangerous–I choose to dismantle these rounds.

2. Taper crimp.

9mm like other automatic pistol cases utilize a taper crimp. This crimp allows cartridges to headspace on the case mouth. It basically removes the case belling. In the process it lightly swages the case mouth and part of the case body into the bullet to provide a tight grip on the bullet. The post crimping case mouth diameter of .378" will also maintain an adequate case mouth edge for headspacing.[19c]

A proper taper crimp function must be sufficient to withstand a 35 pound push or pull and not have the bullet move in or out to meet SAAMI specs.[64] To estimate a 35 pound push test, press a loaded round onto a bathroom scale until the dial reaches over 35 pounds. If this pressure does not push the bullet into the case—you are likely good to go.

3. Power factor.

When loading 9mm for short range target and plinking, the lowest powder charge that will cycle the slide is often all you need. However this caliber is very popular in competitions—especially the Production division in USPSA. In this competition you need to meet a minimum force of your reloads. This is called power factor(pf) and there is a "minor" and "major" class. Power factor is a function of bullet weight and velocity. The equation reads—bullet weight in grains X velocity in fps divided by 1000. The lowest power factor(pf) allowed in USPSA is 125 and this is called "minor".[6r]

For example: A 124 grain 9mm bullet at 1010 fps will equal a power factor of 125. Increase the velocity to 1073 fps and the power factor goes up to a pf of 133. This latter load (or even higher) is a safer pf if you don't have a chronograph and going to a velocity verified shoot. The velocity of any load can vary in your pistol depending on the barrel chamber and the barrel length. Some articles claim a difference of 50 fps between a 4" and 5" barrel. Don't go to a sanctioned match without testing your round on a chronograph or load your ammo to a pf of at least 140–if you cannot make minor at the match your score will not be counted.[6r]

Reaching a pf of 165 for "major" in 9mm is a real problem and will be discussed in Chapter 11–new powders.

4. Sticking cases. The 9mm case is so small and light that it tends to stick to the powder funnel/belling die of the Dillon XL 650. To manage this natural tendency to stick, here are some popular solutions:[6s]

- Control the amount of case mouth belling. The greater the belling, the more the tendency to stick to the funnel. The standard belling is .01" over the sized case mouth and the maximum is .02"

- Spray One Shot case lube in the case mouth and let it dry ten minutes before reloading–especially with new cases
- Polish the powder funnel/belling die
- Avoid wet tumbled cases with stainless steel pins. This removes the natural carbon deposits which act as a lubricant
- Walnut media cleans cases more than corn media and may promote cases sticking
- Clean the expander die. The result of sticking cases leaves horizontal brass particles on the expander die– the lack of cleaning this brass residue will also cause more case sticking
- The varying case lengths of range brass can lead to sticking for cases beyond the maximum case length. Long cases leads to over belling which naturally leads to more sticking.[6s]

5. Primer types. The SPP is generally the standard primer for the 9mm cartridge. Other primers can be used as follows:[7b]

- SMPP. The magnum primer can used as long as you are not loading to or near max load. You can get a 10–50 fps increase in velocity with magnum primer use. These are very popular in cowboy shooting for the ignition of very low powder charges

- SRP. The small rifle primers are the same size as standard small pistol but are harder steel. Will your gun fire them off? Because they are hotter, you should use 10% less powder unless you check them on a chronograph. Some of these SRP approximate the magnum small pistol primers.
- LPP cannot be interchanged with LRP.[7b]

Generally when buying small primers take the standard first despite the brand available. In times of shortages it is very common to take the alternatives–SMPP or last SRP.

6. Powders and bullets.

A–Powders. The choice of powders for 9mm frequently depends on velocity requirements. Low velocity target loads function best with fast burning powders such as Red Dot, Clays or Titegroup(#8–15 on a burn rate chart based on 148 loads). High velocity loads with jacketed bullets function best with slower burning powders such as Power Pistol(#34 on a burn rate chart based on 148 loads).[19d]

After reviewing several manuals, I have summarized some 9mm data on fast burning powders with 124 gr. of lead.[39] NOTE never use reproduced data for reloading–verify your load in your own manual.

Powder	Grains	Velocity fps	COAL	Power factor
Red Dot	3.6	1000	1.13	124
	4.3	1100	1.15	136
Titegroup	3.6	1002	1.125	125
	4.0	1070	1.15	133
Clays	3.0	857	1.15	106
	3.3	1000	1.125	124[39]

As for slow burning powders, Hornady's 9th edition manual states that Power Pistol produced excellent velocity and uniformity with all bullet weights. It is Hornady's number one choice for jacketed bullets.[28d]

Powder	Grains	Velocity fps	COAL	Power factor
Power Pistol				
115gr. FMJ	4.8	1000	1.10	115
	6.7	1250	1.10	144
147 gr. JHP	3.5	750	1.10	110
	5.1	1000	1.10	147[28d]

The fast burning powders make great target loads and can even make "minor" class. Clays has an extremely narrow working range in handgun cartridges–especially in 9mm. A very small increase in powder charge can raise the pressure dramatically(pressure curve is way too steep). Yet 3.0gr. of clays makes a comfortable light target load as long as it cycles your slide. Although you can make "minor" with Red Dot and Titegroup, these powders are snappy. The slower burning powders give more of a push type of recoil with uniform velocities in making "minor".[65]

B–Bullets. All varieties of bullets work well in 9mm.

Jacketed bullets are used with high velocities especially when trying to make "major" power factor. They are also popular as hunting bullets and Hornady makes a fine JHP-XTP hunting bullet for $20 per hundred. Bulk jacketed bullets are available through many sources to include Precision, Delta, Zero and many others.

Coated, plated and moly bullets will be discussed in Chapter 12. Lead bullets make great target bullets. They are available through cbbullets.com and many other manufacturers. A bulk order of CB bullets, 1000–125gr. RN costs $76(free shipping).

A reminder–bullet feeders by RCBS and Hornady require the use of jacketed bullets. Whereas Mr. Bullet Feeder advertizes that their bullet feeder can be used with jacketed, plated, coated and lead bullets but lead bullets need some modification with powdered mica.

7. Flyers.

When you just finished shooting a full magazine and you step up to the target, you suddenly find one or two hits way out of a tight group. You wonder what happened since you loaded all these rounds the same way. Why am I getting the occasional flyer? Here are some causes:[7c]

- Human error is always the number one cause. If you don't believe it, shoot your gun in a ransom rest!
- The first shot tends to be the flyer. Racking the slide manually is not the same effect as the gun loading the other rounds–the lockup is different
- Varied case thickness is common with CBC cases. This is more of an issue with plated and coated bullets
- Varying case OAL affects the crimp which affects accuracy
- Tumbling bullets
- Powder charge consistency
- Uneven bullet bases especially with lead
- Reduced powder charge–you may not be getting enough bullet obturation to seal gases and grab the rifling
- Gun does not like your load
- May slightly be more common with plated/coated bullets?
- Combination of causes
- Operator error–again and again and again![7c]

8. FAQ's regarding 9mm.

FAQ's are a popular method of presenting multiple issues that only require a one paragraph answer or less. They cover the most frequently asked questions that cover this caliber and the use of the Dillon XL 650.

A–Why are cases getting under the plate–causing casefeeder jams?

> The small nature of a 9mm case is such that it easily gets stuck under the casefeeder plate. An extra heavy load of cases in the hopper(greater than 400 cases) can angle the plate rearward under the cases and lift the exiting end of the plate. This increases the gap under the plate and allows cases to fall in. Once you have cases stuck under the plate, the motor starts to slow down and can even stop rotating. Stop and remove these stuck cases to avoid burning out the motor. To clear this jam use a hook or remove the plate which requires the emptying of the hopper. The other common cause is a forgotten washer used in magnum cases and left under the plate.[10a]

B–Why will ammo not chamber?

The common cause is a case bulge. Too much heavy taper crimp can bulge the case. Also some firearms do not sufficiently support the base of a case leading to a bulge at the base. The sizing die needs to be close to the shellplate in order to remove this bulge. If it does not relieve it, you need to discard the case or put it thru a G-RX die(previously discussed).[10b]

C–Why do 9mm cases vary?

There are many 9mm case variations to include wall thickness, internal volume, cartridge weight, case length and many more. Most reloaders feel there is no value in separating cases by brand. Yet sorting is done if loading at max pressure, need the best accuracy or loading self defense loads.[66] Here are some specifics:[10c]

- PMC makes cases with extra thick walls which may increase case longevity but may cause chambering problems in some guns
- Remington has a variance in weight which may cause a variance in neck tension
- Primer pockets are tighter in S&B cases

- Federal cases seem thinner and so do better with lead which are .001" larger than jacketed bullets
- Some 9mm cases have a different profile at the head and the extractor may not extract them in some guns
- Range picks often have military cases with crimped primer pockets that need crimp removal or discarding.[10c]

D–Why are bullets seating crooked?

The major cause is a bullet not started straight. Using your fingers to hold and guide the bullet is often done–but if the belling is done properly, this should not be necessary. The case mouth belling should be .01-.02". The sized case mouth is .377-.379" and so the proper belled case mouth should be at least .387-.389" to a maximum of .397-.399". A crooked insertion may not be easily recognized–the normal "wasp waist" appearance at the base of the bullet has to be uniform all around the cartridge to have a straight insertion. This will allow you to notice the defect before it fails to chamber in your gun.[10d]

E–Why are fired cases black?

The powder charge and resulting pressure is too low to expand the case around the chamber. This causes gases to come back and deposit soot along the case body. It is possible that this round will not cycle the slide backwards. This is frequently encountered when working up a load and using the lowest powder charge in the manuals.[10e]

F–Is it dangerous to seat bullets deeper than the suggested COAL?

If a full power load(35,000 psi) using a fast burning powder is seated 0.1" deeper, the pressure will increase to 70,000 psi when fired. This is extreme seating but even seating .01" deeper will result in excessive pressures. It is clear that these excessive pressures can damage the gun or the shooter.[64]

9. My 9mm reloading experience.

Years ago I reloaded 9mm on a Square Deal B. Now 30+ years later, I had the opportunity to again reload 9mm for the Ruger American Pistol. With all the experience I had accumulated loading the 38 sp. and 44 mag., I quickly realized that loading a small automatic case presented its own set of peculiarities. I had to relearn and adjust techniques to meet the challenge. Here is the result:

A–Cases. I purchased 1500 range pick cases and chose my six favorite headstamp–Fed, Win, RP, Hornady, Blazer and Speer. I discarded many foreign headstamp with the exception of GFL and Perfecta. These are made by Fiochi but manufactured in Missouri and sold at Walmart. I discarded all military crimped primer pockets. Other than visualizing the crimped pocket, these headstamps usually say GAL or have a series of numbers–they never say 9mm Luger as most commercial headstamps reveal.

The final tally after sorting is as follows:

Favorite six American headstamp	1200
GFL/Perfecta	150
Discarded military	75
Other discarded cases	50
Other tried cases(CBC & PMC)	25

I then proceeded to reload the 6 favorite headstamps and the CBC/PMC cases with 1100 125 gr. RN lead and 100 Hornady 147 gr. XTP-JHP. I saved the GFL/Perfecta cases for a future time.

B–Press modifications. I installed a HIT Kit and was amazed how the shellplate was tight to the platform. It rotated smoothly without the "end kick"–there was no flipping of powder out of the cases.

C–Components.

Powder–Titegroup 3.8 gr.

Primers–CCI small pistol

Bullets–Lead 124 gr. RN COAL 1.125" per Hodgdon manual 147 gr. XTP-JHP COAL 1.10" per Hornady manual

D–Stage by stage points of interest.

<u>Casefeeder.</u> No case found its way under the rotating plate. There was one "dam" blockage in the casefeeder old style triangular funnel. One case entered the casefeeder tube upside down. Two missed 40 caliber cases entered and plugged the casefeeder tube. Otherwise there were no other problems encountered in the casefeeder assembly.

<u>Stage-1 Sizing.</u> Special attention needed to fit the sizing die as close to the shellplate as possible–close but not touching. The length of the 9mm case makes sizing an easy process with little resistance.

<u>Stage-2 Belling/powder drop/priming.</u> As I was using a new Dillon 3-die pistol set, the cases were sticking to the belling die. I polished the die with 320 grit sand paper and progressed to 800 grit with resolution of the sticking cases. I did notice that some CBC cases were still sticking to the die since the metal is known to be thicker–these cases were then discarded.

The priming at this station was easy and smooth using

CCI primers. I only had four high primers. There were no issues with powder dropping using 3.8gr. of Titegroup.

Stage-3 Powder check. Since the powder metered well, there were no charges that triggered the alarm. Also there were no "high stepping" cases found in this batch.

Stage-4 Seating. With a case belling of .015" over sizing, the lead bullets from CB Bullets were seated with minimal to no lead shaving. The COAL uniformity was easily maintained.

Stage 5 Crimping. The taper crimping removed all belling and left the case mouth/neck .002" smaller than the sized diameter. The crimped case ejected smoothly to the bin and did not bind on the ejection wire which had been altered per directions to fit the HIT Kit.

E–Cartridge gage rejects. As I started loading, I would check the loaded rounds in the EGW chamber checker and even a few rounds with the barrel "plunk test". After a dozen cases I felt good to go and would check a full 7 hole EGW chamber checker every one hundred rounds.

After all 1000 lead rounds were loaded, I checked each round in the 7 hole EGW checker. The result is that I found 27 cartridges that did not properly fit in the chamber checker. These were high rejects that did not go flush to the top of the checker. The 27 rejects were by these headstamps:

CBC–9	Win–9	PMC–1	Hornady–1
Fed–3	RP–2	Speer–1	Blazer–1

Four of these 27 rejects also had a high primer and one had an inverted primer. The one inverted primer was a pleasant surprise considering that I had just added an adjustable rheostat to my RF–100.

The other finding in this 1000 round check was 8 rounds that fell below the checker's flush point. To my surprise these rounds were actually 380 cal. cases that got reloaded along with the other 9mm cases–they were not detectable among the 9mm cases.

IMHO–When processing a new range pick batch of cases, it is wise to check each round in a chamber checker. The 380 rounds above would have fallen deep in the gun's chamber and would have misfired as well as failed extraction–not a good situation during competition.

CHAPTER – 9

MY EXPERIENCES

PS-Enjoy this chapter, it does not have technical data!

MY SHOOTING HISTORY

My shooting history goes back thirty five+ years and my competitive shooting history encompassed twenty of those years. Here is a progressive chronology of my shooting experience which will give credence to my accumulated theory and practical experience. Even before I started competing there was a need for volume reloading with a progressive press. My two teenage sons would load a batch of 9mm, go to the neighborhood range, and return to reload another batch and so on. Meanwhile I was busy ordering more components. Those were the days with the Dillon Square Deal B.

Years later after retirement I started competing in Cowboy

Action Shooting(CAS), long range Buffalo shoots, and later USPSA. Long range Buffalo shoots involved a 4X6 foot steel buffalo at 600 yards. I was shooting a Pedersoli sharps model 1874 in 45–70 and using black powder with open vernier sights. I recall a yearly big shoot when I hit the buffalo 5 out of 6 shots. I lost 1st place because someone else also hit the buffalo 5 times but did it 20 seconds faster!!! I did not know it was a timed match. I soon realized that long range shooting was not my style–I needed a faster sport and one with much more shooting–CAS.

I competed in Cowboy Action Shooting in Vermont from 1996 to the present. CAS in Florida from 2008 to 2013. USPSA in Vermont from 2000 to 2009 and Florida from 2002 to 2009. The firearms I used in CAS were: the Ruger New Vaqueros revolvers in 38, Uberti model 1873 rifle in 38 and Stoeger double barrel 12 gage shotgun. The firearms I used in USPSA were: Kimber 1911 in 45acp(limited 10 and steel challenge), Glock model 17 in 9mm (production), and S & W 686 with moonclips for revolver division.

While shooting CAS in Florida, we had a yearly two day shoot. This was the big shoot of the year with many out of town shooters. In 2012, I won first place in silver senior division(age 65–69) The last year I competed in Florida, I registered in the Cowboy division(any age) where shooters had better vision, reflexes and physical speed. By changing division, many shooters thought I was wasting my chances of placing again in silver senior class. When trophies were awarded, I won 2nd place in the Cowboy class–with an accolade that will never leave me.

It was during those early competitive years that I had a tremendous need for volume ammo. When you start a competitive shooting sport at age 55, you need to practice regularly to overcome the edge of the younger shooting competitors. The learning curve and muscle training can only be achieved with long and frequent shooting sessions. Consequently I dedicated many hours reloading 1200–1800 rounds to shoot two or three 600 round practice sessions per week. It was during these early years that I upgraded my Square Deal B to the Dillon XL 650–and shortly thereafter a second XL 650 for Florida.

It was clear that by 2000 my shooting and reloading activities were now my "hobbies". As busy as I was, I also participated in the shotgun shooting sports to include trap, skeet, and sporting clays–which meant more reloading sessions. The cost of buying all loaded ammo to do this kind of shooting was intolerable. This is when I got into smelting wheelweights, casting bullets and 7 ½ shot. More info on casting in the last section of this chapter.

After those prime years of shooting, age started to creep up. I noticed changes in vision, reflexes, speed and memory/motivation. It was time to streamline my shooting activities. The first activity to go was smelting, casting and shot production. The long hours spent at these tasks was taking its toll. The last year spent at casting provided a large surplus of shot that lasted 5 years. The extra bullets lasted only one year. I then started to buy bulk orders of bullets. The cost was initially minimized by selling on E-bay my smelting, casting molds, lube equipment and shot maker.

The second activity to go was USPSA. As I moved on in age, it was difficult to keep up with some physical antics such as going prone, dropping to your knees, crawling thru obstacles etc–all while your firearm is hot and on the clock. It was clear that the membership was changing age to the 20–40 age group. The firearms were moving more towards super race guns and leaving the revolver at the wayside.

The next activities to leave were: steel challenge, skeet and sporting clays. This left CAS and trap. Trap shooting is a long tradition of weekly local shoots for pleasure–with friends. CAS was evolving into an older group of participants as compared to USPSA. CAS became my sole competitive sport and I was fortunate to have two ranges within my driving reach for day shooting events. As mentioned above, I retired from CAS in Florida in 2013. I continued to compete for three more years in Vermont but in 2016 I started to shoot JFF(just for fun). Shooting JFF is a completely new approach to shooting. It provides the pleasure of shooting without the stress and tension to perform. JFF provides an avenue for the aging shooter to stay in the shooting sports.

Throughout all these years of shooting, I documented all my purchases of primers. In 2007 my total was 250,000 primers purchased. I stopped counting in 2007 which was also the end of my heavy training years. I can only guess what my count is some ten years later.

"That's the way it was and I am sticking to it"

MY PISTOL RELOADING SESSIONS

I am a hobby reloader. I enjoy the activity and it drives me to return to it as often as possible. Consequently I space out and limit each reloading session to 600 rounds and keep "mega" all day reloading events to a minimum. Frequent reloading sessions help us recall our abilities–we all forget when we don't reload regularly.

During my competition training years, I set up a reloading routine that matched my shooting practices. A standard week included four days dedicated to training. I had three practices of 600 rounds and reloading sessions of 600 rounds the same day as the practices. The fourth day, I had a loading day of 1200 rounds–if needed. I tried to maintain three days per week for home chores, family and social events.

Prior to a reloading session was my prep time. I would load primers using the Dillon RF–100 into 5 tubes plus the magazine tube of the XL 650. Other prep activities include: retouching the lubrication points of the press, cleaning the dies of lead shavings and other debris, polishing brass from the last shooting session, selecting the powder and bullets. When loading large pistol cases(45 long colt or 44 magnum) I would spray the cases with "one shot" and let them dry. If I decapped live primers I would put on safety glasses and ear plugs. I also included reviewing my inventory of loading components—to bulk order before running out.

The final prep work was to set the press for the powder charge, seating depth, crimping adjustment and powder check for the bullet and powder type. Doing this stage ahead of the actual reloading session was the most efficient use of reloading time. Frequently each subsequent reloading session used the same components and so this final stage could be skipped. The press setting of powder charge and dies was best done by deactivating the priming and case feeding system. I removed the frame priming cam and deactivated the casefeeder by placing a 223 case beside the case feed arm—as previously described. At the end of prepping, the powder went back into the container but the primers were left in the magazine tube.

My ritual when starting my reloading session is as follows:

- Place safety glasses on
- Oil the upper and lower cycling ram. Cycle three times and wipe off the excess
- Turn off radio, tv and tumbler

- Add a full hopper of powder and tap the hopper to get the powder under the baffle
- Manually cycle the priming arm to move the primer to the spot ahead of the priming punch(+- 7 cycles)
- Add +- 350 cases of 38 or +- 400 cases of 9mm to casefeeder hopper and start the casefeeder motor on low
- Add a case to station one
- Check buzzer on priming system and powder check
- With your bullets handy, start reloading
- Check the powder charge for the first +-10 rounds or till you see reproducibility of the powder charge

With a reloading session in progress, you need to add the following steps.

- Add primers by the full primer tube(100)
- Clean dies every 300 rounds when loading lead bullets
- Check the powder charge every 100 rounds assuming you have a powder check in place
- Add powder when the hopper level gets to half
- Add brass after 300 rounds
- Empty the ammo bin every 100 rounds unless you have a dam at the end of the bin

- Oil the upper and lower cycling ram every 300 rounds
- Lubricate the indexer ring every 100 rounds at the indexer block and the ring itself every 600 rounds
- Make whatever calls need to be attended to as well as other activities before restarting to reload

Once the reloading session has begun, I do my best to stay focused–yet interruptions do occur such as an important phone call, a visitor and so many more. When interruptions occur, I follow this rigid approach–I finish the ram cycle and prime the next case at station two and STOP. By sticking to this routine, I know that on my return to reloading, the first thing I always do is to add a bullet to station 4 and restart reloading by cycling the ram. This method avoids mistakes.

Variations of any routine is a human trait. There are times when a reloading session has to be doubled to produce 1200 rounds. There are commitments and events that can keep you from your reloading center. These are the times that you have to be careful and well focused at the task at hand. To start a second 600 round reloading session, you need to load 6 tubes of primers, oil the upper and lower cycling ram, lubricate the indexer ring/back/block and follow the other steps of a session in progress. Beyond these single and double reloading sessions, I occasionally had rare "mega" reloading sessions on those boring rainy days. Although those "mega" reloading sessions are in the past, I recall the need for a reserve of loaded rounds in my early competitive years. I was younger, more focused, more motivated, had more stamina and was very secure in the operation of the press. After working the reloader on and off for 8 hours, I generated +-3500 rounds. IMHO, that was foolish and would strongly discourage anyone from attempting this activity.

Finally at the end of my single or double reloading session, I perform my closing routine.

- Run the primers out of the priming magazine tube
- Manually remove leftover cases in the case feed hopper
- Run the cases out of the casefeeder tube
- Empty the powder measure and return the powder to its container
- Clean your dies and your reloading bench
- Verify that the case feed motor is turned off

This reloading routine has served me well. It is an efficient use of time, it has a comfortable pace and it is a non pressured event. I can easily load these 600 rounds over one+ hour from start to clean up—a double session also can be achieved in 2.5-3 hours without rushing. Although this is my routine, you must adjust it to fit your needs. I am certain that many of my steps will also be part of your routine.

MY RIFLE RELOADING SESSIONS

Unlike the regular occurring pistol reloading sessions, rifle reloading occurs twice a year and often done in batches. The first occurs in the spring and involves loading rifle for target shooting and the second occurs in the early fall when I reload rifle hunting loads.

The target rifle loads include loading 30–30 cases with lead gas check 170 grain bullets from "Trueshot", and use reduced rifle loads(more in Chapter 13). The shooting events involve shooting freestyle at steel plates at 50 and 100 yards– the plates ring like a bell. These rounds are loaded by the same method as hunting loads below.

The rifle hunting loads are produced as a separate reloading session. I reload for myself, two sons and two grandsons and in four rifle calibers: 30–30, 7mm–08, 270 win, 30–06 and one pistol caliber–44 magnum loaded during my pistol reloading session. For rifle I use RCBS dies and use two presses–Lyman turret and Dillon XL 650.

I start by ordering bullets for the four rifle calibers–all Hornady and a box of 100 for each caliber. The 30–30 bullet is the "flex tip" with cannelure for use in tubular magazines. The other three are the interlock–sst type with a polymer tip and cannelure. All four bullets are the boattail design which eases the seating stage and does not necessitate the use of an M die.

My prep day consists of polishing all 400 cases since they have been sitting for months. I check all new range brass for primer pocket crimps. I place 100 rounds of one caliber in 4 different loading blocks. This allows me to spray the front, back and neck of each case. I spray the Dillon case lube at 45 degrees to allow some lube to enter the case mouth. I start loading the 30–30 first since it is the easiest caliber to load. It has a slightly tapered body as compared to the three other calibers and its short case length promotes easier full length sizing. I load this caliber in two batches. First I perform full length sizing and decapping. I can quickly determine if the amount of lube is adequate before I get to the other three more difficult calibers. Full length sizing and decapping is performed on the Lyman turret. IMHO, I do not size on the Dillon XL 650 because I feel the cycling mechanism and shellplate are not strong enough to withstand the forces needed to do full length sizing. In comparison the turret press is a rugged system capable of easily forcing these long rifle cases into the sizing die and then pull out without getting stuck. The Lyman turret has a "cam over" system in the cycling arm that allows you to have the sizing die as low as possible on the shellholder. This produces maximum sizing of the case. Using the Dillon spray lube and this turret press, I have never had a stuck case.

The next step is to manually wipe each case to remove the lanolin of the Dillon lube–using a towel soaked with alcohol. The alternative method of removing the lanolin is to wipe them off after the round is fully loaded or place the loaded round in a tumbler with clean corn medic treated with a tablespoon of mineral spirits for 10 minutes(as previously discussed).

The final step involves the last three stages—priming, powder charge and seating/crimping. This is performed on the Dillon XL 650. I have a toolhead for each of the four rifle calibers. Each toolhead has: powder die/funnel and seating/crimping die for each caliber. I did not purchase four different conversion kits. Instead I found that several of the parts fit more than one caliber. For examples the 308 shellplate also fits 30–06 and the 7mm–08. The 30 caliber funnel fits the 30–06 and 30–30. The 270 funnel fits the 7mm–08. Universal parts allowed me to have four preset toolheads for a caliber specific powder funnel and seating/crimping die.

Very few casefeeder modifications were needed to accommodate each caliber. Once the seating/crimping is adjusted for each caliber, the only thing that needs to be done when changing calibers is to set the powder measure for the charge.

The final sequence goes as follows. Station 1 is for adding a case to the shellplate from the casefeeder. Station 2 is for priming with a large rifle primer and adding the specific powder charge. Station 3 is the powder check. Station 4 is the combined seating/crimping. Station 5 is open. If you use separate seating and crimping dies then you would use Station 4 and 5. See below for variations in loading 30–30.

I do not prime on the turret press because of the complete facial exposure in case of a primer explosion. The turret aluminum primer feeding tube which holds 50 primers seems to point at the operator and the tube is not contained in a steel sleeve. With the Dillon XL 650 the operator is semi protected from station 2 by the large frame of the press located between station 2 and the operator, and the primer magazine tube is contained in a steel sleeve.

After loading 100 rounds of one caliber and removing the lanolin, I restart the process with another caliber and reload the next 100 rounds in two batches–sizing/decapping on the turret and finalizing on the Dillon.

A variation of my method is feasible. Some reloaders like pure batch reloading. In this case you would lube and size/decap all 400 cases in the first sitting. I have done this and found that the drawback was a sore arm and shoulder from cycling the arm for 400 cases consecutively!

The 30–30 hunting loads are loaded with some specific variations. I use a separate seating die at station 4. The crimping die I use is the Lee Factory Crimp die set at station 5(as discussed in chapter 6).

There is no perfect system but this double batch system works well for me. I can plan to reload as many calibers per session as I wish. Limiting each batch to 100 rounds prevents operator fatigue and prevents errors in mixing calibers. This method allows me to set up for one caliber and complete the loading before changing to another caliber. As usual, you can modify my system to fit your needs.

MY CASTING YEARS

Designing a training program for three shooting sports lead to a shocking reality check. It was clear that shooting 25,000 rounds per year was not sustainable financially even at year 2000 rates. A source of bullets with low cost was necessary or the idea of a training program had to be abandoned. The answer was clear—make your own bullets and shot. This started a cascading series of events.

STAGE 1–SMELTING.

I started gathering wheelweights from local garages and tire shops. I traveled as far as 50 miles and gathered large amounts of wheel-weights. My cost in 2000 was $15–20 for a 5 gallon pail weighing 225 pounds. The wheelweights were dumped on the cement floor of my shed and shoveled into coffee cans for transfer to the smelting pot. I used two 6 quart cast iron pots fitted to two burners—a cooking gas stove and a high btu turkey cooker. The high btu unit sounded like a roaring jet engine and would melt three pots of wheelweights to one of the low btu cooking stove. The molten lead was then poured into cast iron cupcake molds to make ingots for future use. The smelting phase was performed outdoors on a clear day with little wind to push fumes in your face–or taking advantage of prevailing winds to push fumes away. I also had a high fan above my head to push fumes and smoke away from me.

It was a hard day to fill the pot, strip away the wheelweight metal clips, flux the pot with sawdust when there was oil on top of the lead, pour the liquid lead into the molds, transfer the cooled ingots to their storage area and restart the process.

After this initial smelting session(one of many) it was time to start making bullets and shot. I purchased Lyman's handbook on casting and searched the web for more info. I then purchased the casting equipment:

- I started using a friend's bottom pour furnace and eventually purchased a Lee bottom pour unit
- Lyman 4 hole molds for 125 gr. TC 38 special, 230 gr. RN 45 acp. and 240 gr. RNFP 44 special
- Lyman lube and bullet sizer with base heater and sizing dies
- Red rooster hard lube
- Midway flux and drop out
- Littleton shot maker
- Many assorted tools of the trade

A full 5 gallon pail of wheelweights yielded 175 pounds of ingots. Doing the math I could load 5300-45acp 230 grain bullets or 9700-38 sp. 125grain TC bullets from 175 pounds of ingots. For those who need proof–using the 125 gr. bullet there are 56 bullets to the pound(7000/125) and 18 pounds to the 1000 bullets(1000/56). At 18 pounds to the 1000 bullets then there are 9700(175/18) bullets per 175 pounds of ingots. As far as 12 gauge shotgun shells, each round has 1 1/8 ounce of shot(1.125 ounce). Each box of 25 shells has 28 ounces of lead or 1.75 pounds of lead. 175 pounds of ingots would yield 100 boxes of shotgun shells.

STAGE 2–CASTING.

The ingots were melted in my bottom pour furnace and the 4 hole molds were filled. Bullets were dropped on a bed of towels to prevent deforming the hot bullet. Defective bullets and the sprue were added to the melt. The goal was to produce anywhere from 1500 to 2000 bullets per 4 hour time frame. Casting was performed in my shed but inside the overhead doors–away from rain. I also had a fan above my head to push the fumes outside.

STAGE 3–LUBING.

All these lead bullets need hard lube added to the lube groove and need to be sized. Using a Lyman lube and bullet sizer, a sizing die was chosen for each bullet and the hard lube was pre heated. Each bullet had to be applied to the machine, the cycling arm processed and the lubed and sized bullet exchanged for another. You had to concentrate and could not dawdle if you wanted to process the bullets cast in stage 2. My best time was to process 1000 bullets in 1.5 hours!

So here come the bean counters. Is it really worth the time and effort to produce 2000 bullets in 6–7 hours? Well in 2000 a 1000 bulk ammo purchase was +- $75 or +- $150 for 2000 rounds. My cost was less than $25 for wheelweights and propane. My time expenditure was quite long. When you are retired and living on a fixed income your time is worth nothing. What is important is to minimize your monetary outlays for your hobbies–in reality we do this because it is a hobby.

Retrospectively–If I was to cast bullets in the future, I would do volume lubing. I would have a separate vibratory tumbler and add "moly" powder and lube 1000 automatically in minutes. More on "moly" lube in Chapter 12.

STAGE 4 CASTING SHOT.

Training for the shotgun sports was a slow process. You could not go to the range and practice. You had to go to a trap, skeet or sporting clays range to shoot. Each of these events required traveling +-50 miles and one could only shoot 100 rounds per event. At this rate it took me a year to shoot +-2500 rounds. However my shooting skills improved tremendously.

The Littleton shot maker was a fantastic machine(still available today). I quickly mastered the machine and the process. I then proceeded to turn 175 pounds of ingots into great looking # 7½ shot.

After this year of shooting the shotgun sports, I decided that it was not feasible to continue this training because of the mileage involved. I then proceeded to make more shot and ended up with two 5 gallon pails of shot that lasted me many years for shooting "trap" weekly at the local range. I then sold the shot maker and moved on to training only in CAS and USPSA.

STAGE 5 LATER YEARS.

The day a commercial bullet maker came to town, I sold all my casting equipment but not the smelting tools. This bullet maker needed lead and I had my regular customers for wheelweighs. I continued smelting and made 10 pound ingots using a mold from Magma engineering. For years I exchanged lead ingots for bullets in all my calibers. This was a great bartering situation for both our benefits. At times I was making extra ingots for wholesaling to the bullet maker.

Over these years of handling lead for smelting and casting, my lead levels were always less than 7mcg/dl. I attributed this to proper ventilation, gloved hands, proper skin care etc. The most important feature for smelting was to take advantage of the prevailing winds to dissipate the smoke and fumes. Other safety features are mentioned in Chapter 13.

In closing this section, it is obvious that casting lead bullets was a very necessary process to maintain such extensive training programs. It is also clear that making bullets manually is a very time consuming activity. I found the entire sequences in producing good bullets very enjoyable. It is true that I spent at least 3+ weeks a year in this labor intensive hobby, but it allowed my other hobbies–shooting and reloading.

RUGER AMERICAN PISTOL(RAP)

1. RAP features and specifications.

A–Size

B–Striker fired

C–Caliber choices

D–Barrel cam

E–Sights

F–Steel barrel

G–Recoil

H–Safety

I–Cocking

J–Trigger

K–Slide lock

L–Grip

M–Magazines

N–Take down

O–Chassis

P–Accessory rail

2. Special features.

3. Negative reviews.

4. Positive reviews.

5. My shooting experience and accuracy testing.

One of my sons recently purchased a Ruger American Pistol(RAP) in 9mm. This provided me three opportunities–return to reloading 9mm as described in Chapter 8, review the gun specifications and test the firearm at the range. I reviewed several on line sites that covered this firearm specifications.

I found that the best source was the American Rifleman magazine–an article written by G. L. Horman, 12/29/2011 issue. The other good source was Ruger's home web site on pistols.

1. RAP features and specifications:[40/41]

A–Size. Full size handgun.

B–Striker. It is a hammer free striker fired polymer frame pistol.

C–Caliber. Comes in 9mm and 45 acp. It meets military and duty firearms specifications.

D–It has a barrel cam designed to reduce felt recoil. This is accomplished by controlling rearward movement of the slide on firing. This cam along with a light slide also reduces muzzle flip.

E–Sight. The rear sight is a metallic Novak fixed sight low mount duo white dot system dovetailed in the slide. The front sight is a single post with a white dot and also dovetailed in the slide.

F–Barrel. It is stainless steel and has six land and groove rifling. Can handle jacket, lead, coated and plated bullets.

G–Recoil. The recoil assembly consists of a flat spring on a guide rod and the entire assembly is made of steel.

H–Safety. The trigger is in two parts–a smooth face and a central trigger safety lever requiring the trigger to be fully depressed for firing. Ruger has recently added to the RAP an external safety lever. This is in response to the push from restrictive states, safety conscious shooters and law enforcement. The new safety is ambidextrous and located on the rear portion of the frame.[42/43]

I–Cocking. When the slide is cycled, the striker is set into a fully cocked position.

J–Trigger. The trigger only has to release the sear by giving it a short and crisp trigger pull.

K–The slide lock and magazine release are both ambidextrous.

L–Grip. The grip and polymer frame are formed from a block glass-filled with nylon. This accounts for the light frame. The grip is ergonomically designed to fit a variety of hand sizes. It comes with three interchangeable wrap-around grip modes. The largest mode has a generous palm swell with a trigger reach of 2.85". The medium grip has a more moderate palm swell with a trigger reach of 2.75". The small module has a nearly straight profile and a trigger reach of 2.55".

M–Magazines. There are two 17 round nickel–teflon plated steel magazines that are of the double stack design.

N–Includes good take down instructions for a simple procedure.

O–Chassis. Has a single piece chassis to support the slide instead of old styles multi piece supports.

P–Rail. It has an accessory picatinny rail with four slots. Located below the frame and in front of the trigger guard. This rail can accommodate a light or a laser sight.[40/41]

2. Special features.

There are special features worth discussing. There is a great article in the "Truth about Guns" forum by Jeremy S and titled "Gun review: Ruger American Pistol" 1/5/2016 [44]. The chosen features are"

- You can run this pistol almost dry. The owner's manual suggests only 4 drops of oil. That is because the stainless steel slide, chassis and trigger are all nitrided and the other stainless steel parts are nickel-teflon plated.

- The removable chassis is one of the best features of this firearm. This chassis is milled from billet– not stamped steel This is one reason the chassis is stamped extended use and +P rated.

- The slide has serrations only at the pistol's rear. These serrations are grippy yet easy on the fingers.

- Field stripping can be done without pulling the trigger.

1. With magazine out of the frame, lock the slide to the rear.

2. Then flip the take down lever clockwise till it stops.

3. Release the slide and pull it off the front of the frame.

4. To remove the chassis, pull the takedown lever all the way out.

5. Finally pull the chassis up and forward out of the frame.

6. Follow these specific steps to reverse the process.

    - This pistol fits in the mid shelf category of Glocks/M&P/XD class. It is not in the higher priced category of H&K and Sig pistols.

3. Negative reviews.

I spent hours reviewing forums to get a feel of shooter's impressions after shooting this pistol. The negative reviews were rare compared to the positive reviews. These are the three negatives that were a recurring issue.

The first was about the trigger. It has a long trigger pull and a long reset. This makes it non user friendly if you do rapid firing including double taps. It also can make it easy to short stroke the trigger reset.[45]

The second regards the manual safety. If the pistol fits, the safety will not touch your thumb. Try on the three different grips if necessary and choose the grip that fits your hands.[45]

The third is the issue of sights. If you wish to install a different sight you will be surprised. The rear sight nearly falls off the slide after the set screw is loosened. The front sight is another matter–it is dovetailed in the slide. It is a nightmare to remove the front sight and it may need to be cut in half. If all you want is a dot other than white–paint it on.[45] If you wish to use a fiberoptic sight, use a gunsmith who may need to use a sight pusher to remove the front sight.[45]

4. Positive reviews.

There was a preponderance of positive reviews too many to cover in this chapter. One specific that caught my attention was about the sear block. This pistol is "drop safe". Unlike traditional sear block, this sear block prevents the striker from coming forward and hitting the primer unless the trigger is pulled.[45] This is what I call a "silent safety" for if you ever drop your loaded pistol you will appreciate the lack of "bang".

The other comment popular on the forums is a consensus of many shooters who tried a RAP. It was surprising to hear that many shooters could not believe the price and were so pleased with the shooting trial that they would put their pistols aside and order a RAP.

Whenever providing a firearm review, you find yourself expressing other shooter's pros and cons on individual gun features. However a conclusion on a review can be so personal as to be short on credibility. For this reason, I chose two conclusions that were a general reflection of many shooter's forums. One conclusion was from an independent icon–Dillon. The other was from the manufacturer–Ruger.

The first is from Dillon's Blue Press article in the 12/2016 issue–"Ruger's revolutionary platform utilized a recoil-reducing barrel cam with a low mass slide and a low center of gravity. This provided a new shooting experience".[1a] The second is from Ruger–"the RAP has an innovative mechanical design, shoots well, handles recoil well and routine maintenance is easily performed".[45]

Considering all these firearm specifications and these varied opinions, I now present my shooting experience with the RAP.

5. My Shooting Experience and accuracy testing.

The RAP is a 30 ounce economical pistol "Made in USA" by Ruger. In past years I have shot Glocks and 1911 pistols and so I am comparing this new firearm with the old standards.

After I loaded 50 rounds of three different powder charges, I went to the range to determine the best charge for this pistol. Titegroup powder charge for the 9mm is a range of 3.6 to 4.0 grain. So I prepared 50 rounds each of 3.6–3.8–and 4.0 grains.

The large pistol grip fit nicely in my hands. The weight and balance felt natural to me. I learned how to field strip the slide off, clean the barrel and lubricate the 4 points as per manual. I familiarized myself with all the firearm features. The result of shooting the three charges is as follows:

A. 3.6 gr. of Titegroup(+-1000fps). The slide in rearward motion seemed a bit sluggish. Yet it ejected the spent rounds and reset the striker properly. There were no misfires and the ejected rounds went three feet at 90 degrees. The gun jammed once with a stove-top that required locking the slide backward and removing the magazine. All rounds went into battery and the firearm was able to handle rapid fire. My impression– I suspected too light a charge.

B. 4.0 gr. of Titegroup(+-1100fps). The slide went backward very fast and actually seemed to pound the back-stop. Cases ejected some 7+ feet to the right and some 3 feet rearward.

Five cases came rearward and hit me high in the chest! There were 2 stove-top jams. Other findings were the same as the 3.6 gr. charge. My impression—I suspected too hot a charge.

C. 3.8gr. of Titegroup(+-1050fps). The slide was snappy but did not seem to pound the back-stop. The ejected case went +- five feet and slightly rearward. There were no jams and there was 100% extraction. Speed shooting functioned properly and there were no misfires. In general all functions seemed within industry standards.

My impression—it amazes me that a range of only 0.4 grains can make such a difference. This mid range charge seems to be the best functioning one in this pistol. Also worth mentioning, the +- 20 rounds that did not chamber in the case gage(as previously mentioned) all entered the chamber and fired without issues.

The few jams that I had all involved a case that seemed to have a shallow groove ahead of the rim. It appeared that this shallow groove prevented the extractor from properly grabbing the rim. The problem was found in a variety of headstamps. These cases were discarded.

I had no difficulty managing the long setting trigger since I had extensive experience shooting a Glock. I had no problem with the slide hitting the web of my right hand as previously alluded to. I did notice that the slide spring was a bit stiff when manually racking the slide but would probably lighten up with use. The RAP functioned well at the range and handled

115 gr. FMJ, 147 gr. Jacket HP and 124 gr. Lead RN–with no barrel leading. All in all, this pistol was a pleasant shooting instrument. I then loaded a batch of Titegroup 3.8 gr. with 124 gr. RN lead bullets and performed some accuracy testing.

Accuracy testing. The generally accepted accuracy of this class of auto pistols is 1.5 to 3.5 inches at 25 yards–as per many forums reviewed. With my pistol in a solid pistol bench rest, I did some initial shooting at 15 yards. Sighting the front post flush with the top of the rear sight and the top of the front post on the bull's-eye, I was shooting 3/4 inch high and on for windage. The shot pattern held at +-1 inch with the occasional flier caused by the operator. These lead bullets appeared accurate.

Shooting at 25 yards and still on a solid pistol bench rest, I fired many rounds using the same sight picture. The shot pattern opened up to 2 inches with about 10% of the shots as wide as 2.5 inches with some wide fliers. I could not determine if the 2.5 inch shots were caused by the firearm or the operator. The wide fliers were certainly operator errors.

After sending 100 rounds down range for accuracy testing, it was clear that the pattern mentioned above was reproducible. I then started shooting free style at 15 yards. My target was a dangling ½ gallon milk jug. Shooting any new gun takes some practice to get comfortable and develop some accuracy. Eventually I got on target and enjoyed shooting at the reactive targets. IMHO plinking is most enjoyable using reactive targets(either steel or milk jugs). Shooting paper is for sighting in, establishing accuracy or practicing for competition that use paper targets such as USPSA.

Chapter summary. IMHO, this pistol felt like a "big old gun" that weighed +-30 ounces. This is +- 6 ounces more than a comparable glock 17. Consequently it would not be my choice for conceal/carry. There is no doubt that it would serve well as a duty, defensive or target firearm. It would also place well in competition—the Production class of USPSA, IDPA or Steel Challenge. At the end of my shooting session, I was left with the impression that it was a durable product that would give you unlimited service during long shooting sessions at the range. IMHO "This is another great economical product from Ruger."

NEW POWDERS

Introduction

1. Power Pistol

2. CFE Pistol

    A–Compensators

    B–Major power factor

    C–CFE Pistol specs

    D–Loading 9mm for major

3. AutoComp

4. Trail Boss

    A–Powder characteristics

    B–Metering issues

    C–Max load determination

    D–Load data

5. FMJ vs TMJ vs. JHP

6. New Powder Loads

A–124 gr. lead
B–115 gr. FMJ/TMJ
C–124 gr. FMJ/TMJ
D–147 gr. JHP

Introduction

For years I have been reloading with old standard and proven powders. I started in the late 70's with Red Dot for pistol and shotgun. Then came a new powder that was claimed to be "cleaner"–so I started using Clays and did so for years in pistol and shotgun loads. The next change came when Titegroup was introduced. This time I stayed with Clays for shotgun but did change my pistol loads to Titegroup. This powder added some important Cowboy Action Shooting features. It was a powder that was not position sensitive which was crucial when drawing guns from holsters. It provided economy and uniform ignition with low charge weights. Later in my 44 magnum, I added Titegroup as my target load and H-110 as my hunting load.

I admit I am reluctant to change powders since these powders have served my needs so well. I realize technology changes in cars but the chemistry of powder stays the same. Despite our shortfalls, there are reasons why we change our popular powders.[14b]

- Guns and certain sports have entered the scene that function best with some of the newer powders!
- A big reason is that manufacturers taunt the reloaders by their marketing phrase "new and improved powder"!
- Powder manufacturers are discontinuing certain powders!
- Some of these new powders are more available on the shelf especially during times of powder shortages!
- Manufacturers claim that modern new powders provide higher velocities at lower pressures with less powder![14b]

In reality, some of these new powders do add a new dimension to shooting and reloading. Included in this category are four powders that are presented: Power Pistol, CFE Pistol, AutoComp, and Trail Boss. In preparation I enclose a comparative burn rate chart reproduced from Hodgdon to include 150 powders from fast to slow burning:

Red Dot	8	Power Pistol	33
Clays	10	AutoComp	43
Titegroup	14	CFE Pistol	44
Trail Boss	19	H-110	63
Win 231	29	IMR-3031	79
Unique	31	H-4895	88

1. Power Pistol.

Early in its introduction, this powder established its "niche" that stands today–primarily a high velocity powder that works best in semi- automatic pistols. Hornady's 9th edition manual highly recommends this powder as highly accurate in 9mm and 45 auto. Other powder features include:[11g]

- Fast and consistent burning–a very energetic powder
- Spherical powder that meters well
- It burns hot with low barrel flash
- Ideal for jacketed bullets
- Functions best with less heavy jacketed bullets– heavy bullets have a steep pressure curve with less room for error
- It is not well suited for lead bullets. The problem is that this powder at low charges can still generate velocities over 1100 fps–ideal for barrel leading. If you choose to use this powder with lead, check your velocities with a chronograph or use the more expensive gas checked lead bullets.[11g]

The Hornady 9th edition manual lists the following 9mm Power Pistol data: (goal of a power factor of 125 or greater)

115 gr. FMJ	COAL 1.10"	
4.5 gr.	1000fps	pf 115
6.7 gr.	1250fps	pf 141
124 gr. FMJ	COAL 1.15"	
4.3 gr.	900fps	pf 112
5.7 gr.	1100fps	pf 136
147 gr. JHP-XTP	COAL 1.10"	
3.5 gr.	750fps	pf 110
5.1 gr.	1000fps	pf 147

Note–never use reproduced data as a source of actual reloading data. Use and confirm these loads in your own manual.

IMHO–I have been surveying my 9mm friends and range shooters. It is clear that Power Pistol has a large following among auto pistol shooters. Their second choice is Titegroup. Their claims is that these two powders do the job in auto pistols. Their final usage depends on which powder is available on the store shelves.

2. CFE Pistol.

A–Prior to presenting this powder, a review of compensators is needed. A compensator is a device connected to the pistol muzzle that redirects propellant gases–to counter recoil and muzzle rise during rapid fire. This added muzzle control decreases recovery time between shots and so compensators are very popular in competition shooting.[11h]

Compensators add weight to the barrel which also minimizes barrel jumping. It also works best with light bullets which inherently minimize muzzle rise. Despite all these muzzle rise controls, the blast energy still has to be dissipated and this may increase perceived recoil but with good muzzle control.[11h]

There are two drawbacks with compensator use. The first is that fouling is more of an issue with lead bullets because of the higher velocities that are needed to maximize the amount of gas expelled in the ports. For this reason, jacketed bullets are more of the norm with compensators. The second is the louder muzzle blast especially if shooting under a roof or indoors.[11h]

B–As in compensators, a review of "power factor" is needed before discussing this powder, and this review applies to shooting 9mm.

If you are shooting for pleasure at plinking or paper targets, the lightest load for 124 gr. lead bullets is ideal as long as the load cycles the slide. If you are shooting Production in USPSA you need to make minor(a power factor of 125+) which is usually achieved using fast burning powders as previously discussed. If you wish to make major(power factor 165+) with a 9 mm, you should stay within the maximum load(35,000psi) or just beyond in the +P range(38,500psi).[7e]

IMHO–whether you are shooting minor or major with a 9mm, it is wise to check your load with a chronograph. I have participated in large USPSA matches where all firearms were chronographed. I have seen shooters shocked to find out that their firearm and load did not qualify for the division they requested!

Both "recoil managing compensators" and "major power factor" will likely require the use of a slower burning powder–here enters CFE Pistol powder.

C–CFE Pistol powder. This is a slow burning powder(burn rate 44/150) best suited for major loads. Slow burning powders can push higher velocities but with less pressure. Its use requires a larger charge weight which makes it less economical. As an example, you can load 1944 rounds with a pound of Titegroup whereas you only get 1428 rounds with a pound of CFE-pistol[7e] Other characteristics of this powder include:[47]

- Clean burning with low muzzle flash
- Its spherical shape meters well
- Has a copper fouling eraser capability[47]

CFE Pistol 9mm loads using 125 gr. jacketed bullets with COAL 1.15" to make minor(per Hodgdon Reloading Center).

Weight–gr.	Velocity–fps	Power Factor	PSI
5.1	1118	144	33000

NOTE: This load is below industry max load of 35000 psi

CFE-pistol 9mm load data using a 124 gr. jacketed bullet with a COAL of 1.15" to make major.[7f](per Hodgdon Reloading Center)

Weight–gr.	Velocity–fps	Power Factor	PSI
6.5	1296	160.5	?
7.0	1338	165.9	?
7.2	1380	171.2	?
7.4	1406	174.3	?
7.6	1432	177.5	?

NOTE: These loads are above industry max of 35000 psi!

Never use reproduced data for loading. Check your load in your manual.

As a point of interest, any load with a power factor greater than 170 can cause bulged cases depending on the case brand, numberof reloads and your gun's chamber.[7f] After absorbing the significance of these two charts of load data, it is clear that making major with a 9mm has its own set of issues that deserve some discussion in this next section.

D–Loading 9 mm for major. There are problems reloading a 9mm to make major. The amount of powder needed usually fills the case so much that extended COAL is needed to avoid powder compression. This leads to custom built barrels whose chambers accommodate such extended COAL. Other custom modifications include fully supported chambers, custom feeding ramps and more changes per individual manufacturer to even approach safe operating levels.[71]

These major loads produce such high pressures that are outside of SAAMI specifications and are not for any over the counter 9mm. In addition you need significant reloading experience to achieve safe over max loads. The Brian Enos USPSA forums have extensive information on loading 9mm for major.[71]

Despite these inherent risks, shooters load major and push the limits of their 9mm because of some claimed advantages. The first is that many 9mm pistols provide high capacity magazines that cuts down magazine changes in competition. The second is that aftermarket barrels are available for Glocks that can withstand 9mm major loads–these are much cheaper than custom built barrels. The third regards "brass lost matches". The life-span of a 9mm case loaded to major is +-2 loadings if starting with new brass. To loose your cases after one or two loadings at a sanctioned "brass lost match" is not so painful because of the economical nature of the 9mm case.[71]

If you are planning to load 9mm major, follow these safety tips:[72]

- Load bullets long–COAL is usually 1.225–1.250". This also means using magazines that can handle these extreme COAL

- Use barrels that have fully supported ramps/chambers and can accommodate the extended COAL
- Small rifle primers can be used but with some case flash hole modifications–this one needs to be researched and clarified!
- Build loads whose velocities are confirmed by chronograph
- Watch for signs of excessive pressure
- Stay with one brand of cases–the thicker the metal, the better
- Some shooters us FN bullets to shorten COAL
- The 124 gr. jacketed bullet seems the most popular
- Some shooters use slightly compressed loads to prevent bullet setback and shorten COAL–IMHO I am somewhat suspicious of this one and it needs further investigation.
- Do not use fast burning powders to reach 9mm major
- Some shooters in this category use a pressure software.[72]

Note: The "Quickload" software($150) is a program that works with windows. It helps reloaders understand how changing variables can affect pressure and velocities. It computes the pressure of a load using the variables of bullet weight, type of powder and charge etc etc. This software helps the 9mm major shooter to stay withing +p pressures of 38500 psi(which is the standard in factory self defense loads).[74]

There are 9mm major shooters that load to +p pressures since they are only 3500 psi higher than SAAMI max. The shooters use modern pistols that are rated for +p use. These include many Glocks, M&P, XD and 1911 pistols. Keep in mind that loading +p or higher will shorten the life of your gun.[73]

If you are loading above +p pressures(38500 psi), you would be wise to consider a custom built barrel that is matched to your ammo. In general a major 9mm load is likely to be in the 40,000 psi range and may even be approaching 50,000 psi range depending on many variables.[73]

IMHO. 9mm is a "minor" cartridge. Why make a gun perform outside its normal range–where you are pushing the limits of safety. I shot USPSA Production for years and always made minor using 4.0 gr. of Titegroup to yield a power factor of +- 135. I just cannot see trying to "beef-up" this caliber to major when there are many calibers that easily reach major within SAAMI specs.

3. AutoComp.

The fact that Winchester called this powder AutoComp was the first clue that it was designed for compensated auto pistols. This powder is economical, clean burning, meters well and has a low flash.[48]

Like CFE Pistol powder, it has a perfect burning speed to feed the compensators with a higher volume of gas to control recoil and muzzle flip.[49] Also like CFE Pistol powder it is not an ideal powder for lead, coated or plated bullets.[7g] The one difference I found was that at maximum loads, CFE Pistol showed less pressure signs on primers but also a slight decrease in velocity.[47]

AutoComp minor and major load
data from multiple manuals:

Bullet	powder gr.	fps	psi	power factor
124gr.FMJ	5.2	1120	33,000	+-140(minor)
	6.8	1365	?	+-170(major)

Note: Never use reproduced load data as your load source. Confirm your load in your own manual.

With the burn rates of AutoComp 43 and CFE Pistol 44 there is very little that needs to be added. These two powders are almost duplicates and the only difference to interchange is the charge weights needed to achieve the same velocities. Choosing between the two powders depends whether there is only one type available on the shelf or whether you are a Winchester or Hodgdon fan!

4. Trail Boss.

A–Powder characteristics. Of all the powders added in recent years, this one adds a new approach to reloading. This was the first powder that finally filled the large cases–44 magnum and 45 colt. At standard charges, this fluffy powder produces a large volume per each grain–you can fill the case up to the bullet base but should not compress the powder. Despite filling the cases, it does not generate high pressures.[51a]

It did not take long after its introduction to be picked up by cowboy shooters especially those who shoot the classic 45 colt. Because it fills the case, it is impossible to accidentally double charge a round. This is an important feature for reloaders who reload on a single press, a non indexing progressive press or any press that does not utilize a powder check/lock-out die system.

B–Metering issues. Unfortunately, this powder does not meter well in Dillon presses unless some management maneuvers are followed:[3e]

- This is a large flake powder that does not provide much gravitational packing. Keep the powder hopper 3/4 full
- The small powder bar will deliver 5 gr. or less. For charges greater than 5 gr., use the large charge bar
- Watch out for static clinging even if you use preventive static electricity techniques

- Slow down your stroke so the powder has time to flow
- Some shooters gently tap the powder measure before lowering the loading platform
- Verify that the powder bar travels 100% as it bells the case .01–.02" and that the fail-safe rod wire nut is tight.[3e]

C–Max-Min load determination. To establish the maximum load of any caliber, find where the bullet base to be loaded is located in the case and make a mark on the outside of the case at this location–then fill the case to that mark. Pour the powder onto a scale and weigh–this is your maximum load. The pressure of this maximum load will be below the maximum pressures allowed for this caliber.[50b]

To establish the minimum load, multiply the maximum load by 70%–this is your minimum load and a starting point in developing an accurate load for your gun.[50b]

It is of note that this system of determining a maximum/minimum load also applies to rifle calibers using Trail Boss. Recent years has rekindled the idea of minimal rifle loads for comfort, practice, plinking and training young shooters–along with using lead bullets in rifles. More on this subject in Chapter 13.[50a]

D–Load data. I reproduced from Hodgdon(HRC), the following minimum/maximum Trail Boss load data for both pistols and rifles.

Caliber	gr. fps......psi	gr......fps.......psi
38 sp. Pistol 125gr. lead RN	3.0..753.....11,600	5.3.....952.....13,400
45 acp Pistol 230 gr. lead RN	3.5...658.....11,200	4.5.....761.....15,100
44 magnum Pistol 240 gr. lead SWC	6.0...828.....19,100	7.3.....917.....21,600
45 colt Pistol 250 gr. lead RNFP	4.5...606.....9,000	5.8.....727.....13,000
30–30 Rifle 160 gr. lead FP	6.5...997.....20,500	9.0.....1195....29,100
30–06 Rifle 150 gr. jacketed BT	13.3...1061...14,700	19.0....1477....26,400

NOTE: Never use reproduced data as your loading charge. Check your load in your own manual. Check COAL of these loads in your manual.

5. FMJ vs. TMJ vs. JHP

In our discussion of semi automatic pistols and newer powders, it has become clear that there are four types of bullets–lead, jacketed, coated and copper plated. The last two will be presented in the next chapter. Lead is the most economical, generally a hardcast in the +- 18-22 Brinell scale and kept a velocities less than 1100 fps. Jacketed bullets are the main focus of this section.

It has been well established that barrel leading is caused by the lead bullet base being exposed to the hot ignition gases and high pressures as the bullet travels in the barrel. These hot and high pressure gases melt lead at the base–it is this melted lead that is deposited in the barrel. When a lead bullet is traveling over 1100fps, the base can be protected by a copper gas check cap to prevent barrel leading.[52]

With this explanation of barrel leading, the manufacturers of copper jacketed bullets have not clarified the significance of exposed lead at the base of some jacketed bullets. There are three types of copper jacketed bullets–FMJ, TMJ and JHP. The difference in these three types is based on the location and amount of lead exposure.[52]

TMJ(total metal jacket same as CMJ-complete metal jacket) has a lead core that is completely covered with a copper sleeve from tip to base–providing total coverage of the lead bullet base. JHP(jacketed hollow point) bullets are made by pulling a copper bud over the lead core from base to tip. The tip is open with lead exposed to form the hollow point, but the base is completely covered with copper.[52]

The FMJ name is a misnomer–it is far from being a full or complete metal jacket. This bullet is formed by pulling a copper bud from tip to base. The tip is fully covered by copper but the copper sleeve ends at the edge of the base–leaving the base completely exposed with the lead core.[52]

IMHO: This bullet with an exposed base has produced many varied opinions. Does this bullet act as a jacketed or a lead bullet. If it acts as a lead bullet with a lead base, then can we justify to push the bullet to maximum speeds and expect it to NOT lead our barrels & compensators.

I have reviewed many forums with many different opinions on the subject. The one consensus is that undersized bullets promote leading from hot gases and high pressures on a lead base. Most jacketed bullets are undersized by .001"–that size along with an open lead base bullet may mean trouble for FMJ. Also compensated guns collect lead from use with open base bullets.[51b] This is not the final word on the subject but it certainly will make you cautious when using FMJ bullets.

IMHO: With new powders at higher pressures and velocities, you need to be aware of their effect on your chosen jacketed bullet when building a load to make major. The ultimate result of your choice is whether you are getting barrel and compensator leading–that is what matters.

6. New powder loads.

When reviewing load data for new powders, keep in mind that manufacturers of components may have their own agenda. Hornady manufactures bullets so their 9th edition manual tends to provide load data that matches their own bullets. They use a variety of pistol powders since they do not make pistol powders. In recent years, Hornady has introduced two rifle powders–Superperformance and Leverevolution.[12n]

Hodgdon 2017 annual edition and HRC reflects the fact that they make powders and so many of their loads have Hodgdon powders. The online site HRC also includes IMR and Winchester powders.[12n]

Reviewing the Hornady and Hodgdon manuals, I divided the 9mm load data into four categories–125 gr. lead, 115 gr. FMJ or TMJ, 124 gr. FMJ or TMJ and 147 gr. JHP. Some of these load data have already been presented but are repeated here to compare the differences between fast and slower burning powders.

A–Hodgdon.....125 gr. lead CN.....COAL 1.125

A-Hodgdon.....125 gr. Lead CN.....COAL 1.125

powder	grains	fps	power factor
Clays	2.9	899	112
	3.3	993	124
Titegroup	3.6	1002	125
	4.0	1096	137
CFE Pistol	4.4	1041	130
	5.0	1156	145
Auto-Comp	4.3	1012	127
	4.8	1102	138

B–Hodgdon.....115 gr. FMJ/TMJ RN.....COAL 1.0

The 115 gr. FMJ/TMJ is very popular with 9mm auto pistol shooters because it is an economical and accurate jacketed bullet. You can make minor by loading near maximum load to achieve a pf of 130–140.

powder	grains	fps	power factor
Clays	3.7	1066	123
	3.9	1095	126
Titegroup	4.5	1135	131
	4.8	1158	133
CFE Pistol		1059	122
	5.9	1185	136
Auto-Comp	5.1	1078	124
	5.6	1161	134

Hornady. . . . . 115 gr. FML-TMJ RN. . . . COAL 1.0

Power Pistol	4.8	1000	115
	6.7	1250	144

C–Hornady.....124 gr. FMJ/TMJ RN.....COAL 1.15

This bullet is very popular with target and competition shooters. The HP type is popular with law enforcement and self defense.

powder	grains	fps	power factor
Power Pistol	4.3	900	112
	5.7	1100	136
Auto Comp	4.2	900	112
	4.9	1050	130

Hodgdon . . . . .125 gr. FMJ/TMJ RN. . . . .COAL 1.090

Clays	3.5	1010	126
	3.7	1056	132
Titegroup	4.1	1069	134
	4.4	1136	142
CFE Pistol	4.6	1009	126
	5.1	1118	140
Auto Comp	4.7	1055	132
	5.2	1120	140

It is of note, that at power factors of 130–140 the velocities are all hovering around 1100fps whether you are using fast or slow burning powders. When loading for target or plinking the minimum loads are ideal as long as it cycles the slide.

D–147 gr. JHP.....COAL 1.10 Data from Hornady and HRC.

This bullet is popular with law enforcement, and hikers as protection against small rabied predators.

powder	grains	fps	power factor
Titegroup	3.2	855	126
	3.6	929	137
Power Pistol	4.2	850	125
	5.1	1000	147
CFE pistol	3.7	864	127
	4.2	963	142
Auto-Comp	3.6	827	122
	4.0	916	135

Disclaimer: As I have mentioned after providing load data charts, never use reproduced data as your loading data. Check your load in your own manual.

CHAPTER-12

ALTERNATIVE AND MODIFIED BULLETS

1. Plated bullets

   A–Plating
   B–Belling and crimping
   C–Load data for SP and TP bullets
   D–Prices

2. Coated bullets

   A–Coating
   B–Polygonal barrels
   C–Coating thickness
   D–Specifications
   E–Bullet shaving
   F–Prices

3. Comparing plated and coated bullets

4. Hornady bullets

   A–Interlock
   B–Flex tip
   C–XTP
   D–Prices

5. Moly coated bullets

    A—Definition
    B—Moly characteristics
    C—Special Moly features
    D—Availability
    E—Accuracy
    F—Gun cleaning
    D—Use in bullet feeders

New additions to our bullet inventory other than lead and jacketed bullets are plated, coated and moly bullets. The first two fill a niche to include lower prices under certain velocity restrictions and allow their usage in polygonal barrels. The last provides a new way of lubricating lead bullets.

1. Plated bullets.

These are produced by several manufacturers such as Berry, RMR, Frontier, Extreme and others. For discussion purposes, we will feature Berry bullets.

Berry standard plated bullets are swaged and plated to a final product that is restruck(sized again) and labeled DS(double struck) for accuracy and precision. These standard plated bullets(SP) can withstand velocities up to 1200 fps and are safe in polygonal barrels. They are ideal for indoor shooting with low smoke and low lead exposure. No lube is needed.[53]

A–Plating. The swaged lead core is exposed to tumbling in an electrically charged(electrolysis) bath of high grade copper–to allow the copper to cling to the lead. The longer the lead core tumbles in this bath, the thicker the plating.[53]

The standard pistol bullets have a plating of .001" (SP) which corresponds to the 1200 fps mentioned above. Bullets with a plating of .003–.008" are labeled TP(thick plated) and can withstand velocities up to 1500 fps in pistols. The plating thickness can allow velocities greater than 1500 fps in rifle bullets. For example, the 30-30 plated bullet velocities can reach up to 1900 fps.[53]

B–Belling and crimping. Most people cannot load these bullets to shoot accurately by using standard reloading techniques. Assuming you have chosen the proper plated bullet, you need to vary two areas of reloading–belling and crimping.[90]

Inadequate belling(flaring) of a case mouth will cut the plating of both SP and TP bullets–which will ruin accuracy. The flaring should be slightly greater than achieved in lead and jacketed bullets(.01-.02"), but not to the point that the flared case will not enter other dies.[90]

Proper crimping is crucial with plated bullets. The crimp in auto pistols does not hold the bullet from "setback"–that is the function of sizing and bullet-wall friction. Over crimping will deform any bullet including plated bullets, and may cut the plating. If the plating is cut, this may cause the base cup plating to stay stuck in the chamber causing a jam or worse.[90]

The best crimp for plated bullets in auto pistols is the taper crimp. This crimp should simply straighten the case flare and not cut into the plating. A roll crimp may be necessary in revolvers and rifles to prevent bullet setback. In these situations, use the least amount of roll crimping necessary to minimize plating damage.[90]

Measuring the proper amount of crimping can be somewhat accomplished with a case gage. After repeated passes at crimping to avoid over crimping, a loaded round should fall easily into a case gage. If it is flush with the top and falls freely out of the gage, you have set a full crimp to standards.[90]

C–Load data for SP and TP bullets. It is clear that the powder charges for SP bullets are the same as lead bullets and kept to velocities below 1200 fps. If you cannot find lead loads in your manual, consider purchasing Lyman's 49th edition manual which has a nice array of loads for lead bullets. Another source of lead loads is to use the jacketed data and start at the minimum load and do not exceed the 1200 fps.[53]

Of powders used for lead bullets(Clays, Red Dot, Titegroup and others), let us not forget that Power Pistol is also a popular powder with plated bullets.[67]

As I reviewed the 2017 Hodgdon manual, I found load data specifically targeting Berry hollow base bullets to reach minor with 9mm 124 gr. BERB HBRN TP COAL 1.15".[18d]

powder	grains	fps	power factor
CFE Pistol	4.9	1007	125
	5.5	1120	139
Titegroup	3.6	957	119
	4.1	1057	131

NOTE: Never use reproduce data as your load data. Check your manual.

Berry hollow base bullets are TP and are unique. They generate slightly higher pressures and shift some weight forward allowing more rifling contact with better accuracy. These bullets also obturate better to grab rifling and so are beneficial in large bore and older guns.[16b]

D–Prices. In order to do a comparative review of plated bullet prices, one has to visit the cost of 9mm bulk lead and jacketed bullets.

Bulk lead at CB bullets, 1000 –9mm 124 gr. RN with a Brinell hardness(BH) of 18 costs $76 with free shipping.[54]

Bulk jacketed bullets. Prices at time of publication.

- Hornady/Brownell. 115gr. FMJ, 500 count for $59
- Everglades ammo. 124 gr. FMJ, 3750 count for $299 or 115 gr. FMJ, 4000 count for $299

- Rainier/Cabelas. 124 gr. FMJ RN, 500 count for $52

- Montana Gold. 115 gr. or 124 gr. CMJ, 500 count for $100

Bulk Berry 9mm bullets. As advertised on Dillon Blue Press.[1e]

Bullet type	500 count $	1000 count $
115 gr. RN-DS	49	90
115 gr. HBRN-TP	52	96
124 gr. RN-DS	51	95
124 gr. HBRN-TP	57	106
124 gr. HBFP-TP	57	106
147 gr. RN-DS	60	110[1e]

Why do we consider plated over jacketed bullets? There is a small dollar savings but there is a big savings on the bore of your gun. Jacketed bullets are the most unforgiving as far as rifling is concerned, and will wear out your barrel quicker than lead, plated or coated bullets. If you do volume shooting, the choice is clear![90]

2. Coated bullets.

Coated bullets are another popular lead bullet modification on the market. Like plated bullets, it has joined popularity because of concerns with lead exposure, barrel wear and safety concerns in certain barrels.

A–Coating. The coating called "Hi-Tek" is a polymeric compound free of copper, bonded with acetone and baked onto the lead bullets. The process is repeated once and this forms a tough surface. The bullets are then sized and the diameter of the lead bullet is not affected. These bullets do not need to be lubed–the coating itself is not abrasive and it acts as a lube.[55]

Using an unsized and unlubed lead bullet, you can apply this "Hi-Tek" coating yourself. The coating is commercially available with instructions on proper application and baking. After baking, if the batch smells of burnt electrical wires, it is a sign of inadequate baking.[7h]

B–Polygonal barrels. Polygonal barrels are dimensionally tighter than square cut rifling. This provides good accuracy with jacketed bullets which are generally .001" smaller than lead bullets. Lead bullets tend to build up lead in the forcing cones causing unsafe pressure increases. Plated and coated bullets do not cause a build up of lead in these barrels and so are safe to use in polygonal barrels. The alternative is to purchase an aftermarket barrel from Lone Wolf and others that can handle lead bullets with normal rifling.[9n]

C–Coating thickness. Although a standard thickness of plated bullets is .001", it seems that the coated bullet's thickness varies by manufacturer. The accepted criteria is that the coating can add as much as .002" but the manufacturers resize after cooling to bring the bullet diameter back to their company specs.[11i]

D–Specifications.[7i]

- You can load up to a velocity of 1500 fps in pistols and 1750 fps in rifles
- Less smoke–a benefit with indoor shooting
- Cheaper than jacketed bullets
- The 9mm diameter is .356"–ideal diameter for lead bullets
- Most coatings are over a hardcast lead bullet–BH of 16-18
- There are many manufacturers but 75% include: Bayou, Blue Bullet, Acme, Black Bullet International, Precision BBI, Chey-Cast, Missouri Bullet and SNS Castings.[7i]

An interesting feature of coated bullets is that they are SASS legal and can be used in CAS. Many shooters feel there is less lead splatter from steel targets. Since the bullets come in so many colors, it is wise to choose a bullet that does not use gold to simulate copper jackets. This would lead to unnecessary questions from officials. It is better to choose red or blue and sail through without inspections.[56]

E–Bullet shaving. Shaving the bullet coating occurs during

seating if there is inadequate belling. Proper flaring will avoid scraping off the coating. If using a Dillon press, obtain a Mr. Bullet Feeder powder funnel($35). This funnel expands the case mouth and distal case so the bullet sits down inside the case when you place it. Another similar special funnel is MBF from Competitive Edge.[8f]

Some warning signs that your seating is scraping off the coating includes an increase of smoke and the smell of burning electrical wires.

To prove this is happening, pull the bullet before crimping. Use a bullet puller other than a kinetic hammer which can be a bit traumatic to a coated bullet. Use the GRIP-N-PULL pliers or the RCBS collet bullet puller. Direct visualization of the pulled coated bullet will immediately clarify the issue.[8f]

F–Prices. The bulk prices for 9mm coated bullets from SNS Castings as advertised in the Blue Press are as follows:

Bullet Type	500 count $	1000 count $
115 gr. RN	41	76
125 gr. FP	42	78
125 gr. RN	42	78
147 gr. RN	47	88
147 fr. FP	47	88

It appears that these coated bullets are the same price as lead but are cheaper than plated and jacketed bullets.

3. Comparing plated and coated bullets.

These two bullets are basically modified lead bullets with one of two coatings. Either one of these modifications are quite similar with some few differences listed below.[16c/7j]

- Both are affected by a roll crimp—worse with plated
- Both are accurate—coated more accurate? Needs investigating
- Coated may be a bit cheaper depending on sales
- Plated are easier to reload
- Plated don't smoke—coated have minimal smoke
- Can achieve higher velocities with coated
- May use less powder with coated
- Coated bullets can be used in CAS
- Coated bullets can be made at home.[16c/7j]

4. Hornady bullets.

Over the years, one can easily get comfortable using a certain rifle bullet because of ease of reloading, accuracy and performance in the field. It is a great feeling to rely on your hunting ammo to function well and yield results reliably. The three bullet listed below can easily handle one of New England's large game—deer, bear and moose.

A–Interlock bullets.[28f]

- A weakened upper section of the jacket by inner grooves ensures consistent expansion.
- The tapered jacket thickness is varied for expansion at all velocities.
- One piece core does not separate like divided cores. It retains more mass and energy for deep penetration and large wound channels.
- A cannelure provides an accurate and consistent crimping point. A base with a boattail design for easy seating.
- Interlocking ring. The raised ring is embedded in the bullet core to ensure the core and jacket are locked in one piece during expansion to retain mass and energy.
- The secant ogive design creates a ballistically efficient profile with an optimum bearing surface. This results in lower drag, increased stability, flatter trajectories and great accuracy.[28f]

B–Flex tip bullets.[28f]

The newest item for lever action rifles in many years. This bullet has a flexible polymer tip that is safe to use in tubular magazines. Other characteristics include:[28f]

- It provides a flatter trajectory and higher velocities when used with its new powder, leverevolution
- An interlocking design keeps the core and jacket together to produce deeper penetration and controlled expansion
- It has a bevel base for easy seating without using an M-die
- It has a cannelure to ensure proper seating and heavy crimping–to prevent bullet setback in tubular magazines.[28f]

C–XTP bullets.[28f]

This bullet was designed for self defense, law enforcement and hunting especially with big bore 44 magnum and 45 colt. It features controlled expansion secondary to the six serrations that divide the bullet into symmetrical sections. The resultant controlled expansion is possible at low to high velocities but prevents fragmentation at high velocities. Like the other bullets, it has a bevel base and a cannelure.[28f]

D–Prices.[24/28f].....per box of 100 bullets. These are quality bullets at an economical price. Consumers appreciate that they are usually available through online and retail stores. Their marketing is consumer oriented since these bullets often go "on sale".

Interlock 30 caliber(.308 dia) $28.49

165 gr. SST Boattail with polymer tip

Ballistic coefficient 0.447

Interlock 270 caliber(.277 dia) $26.99

150 gr. SST Boattail with polymer tip

Ballistic coefficient 0.525

FTX 30-30 caliber(.308 dia.) $31.99

160 gr. Flex tip

Ballistic coefficient 0.330

XTP 44 caliber(.430 dia.) $26.49

240 gr. JHP

Ballistic coefficient 0.205[24/28f]

5. Moly coated bullets.

A–Definition. Moly is a long lasting surface lubricant which forms a non conductive dry film which is ideal for high velocities and high pressures.[80] It is composed of molybdenum disulfide, which is an inorganic compound, formed by combining molybdenum and sulfur. It is a silvery black material that looks and feels like graphite. It is widely used as a lead bullet lubricant because of its low friction properties and its adherence to lead.[81]

B–Moly characteristics.[82/83]

- The moly coating under pressure and temperature melds in the pores of the lead and barrel metal–acting as a lubricant
- An ideal bullet for extended shooting sessions/competition.[82]
- It takes 10-20 shots with moly bullets to coat a barrel for velocities to stabilize
- Once the barrel is coated, do not shoot jacketed bullets–it strips off the moly coating
- With moly bullets, there is less barrel heating with repetitive and speed shooting
- If you have a barrel that does not shoot well or walks badly when it heats up–good reason to try moly bullets.[83]

C–Special Moly features. There are two issues that have been extensively studied by the Norma Precision studies. The first is moly's affect on pressure and velocity. If pressure is reduced with moly bullets, velocity will also be lowered. However velocity is not reduced as much as pressure. Therefore, by increasing the charge in theory you can usually get 1-2% higher velocity. In actuality this converts a 1000 fps cartridge to an extra 10-20 fps–really![84]

The second feature is barrel life using moly bullets. The Norma studies showed that barrels retained accuracy more than twice as long when moly bullets were used from the onset.

With reduced friction from the moly coating, this means that the bullet travels further along the barrel before peak pressure is reached. The result is lower wear and improved accuracy.[84]

D–Availability. You can purchase lead bullets already lubed with moly–many manufacturers offer a hard lube or moly at no extra charge. As an alternative, you can coat your unlubed lead bullets yourself, especially if you cast your own bullets. Online retailers sell Lyman Super powder(6 oz. for $20), a super fine powder of molybdenum disulfide. Simply add this powder to a batch of bullets in a dedicated separate tumbler and process according to directions.[83]

E–Accuracy. The ultimate goal when using moly is to see an improvement in accuracy. Generally the better the barrel the fewer the benefits from moly. If you do not see a substantial accuracy improvement, then you may have questionable reasons to use them.[83]

F–Gun cleaning. Before using moly, clean your barrel the conventional way with brushes, solvents and clean patches. Then repeat the process with a copper solvent till patches are clean.[80]

Just because you are shooting moly bullets, you still have to clean your gun. After extensive shooting, check your barrel for signs of excessive fouling–especially if your gun accuracy is falling. Moly can build up "rings" at certain points in the barrel base. If the build up becomes sufficiently severe, then bullets fired through the restrictions will expand the barrel base at these points. This can damage your barrel permanently.[80]

Cleaning your gun of moly is done the usual way with a bronze brush for normal fouling followed by your usual solvent. For heavy fouling use a nylon brush and follow the brushing with several solvent soaked patches. For extreme fouling with barrel rings, use a very stiff nylon brush followed by solvent patches using Kroil penetrating oil as a better solvent. The trick is to remove moly excesses–NOT to strip off all the moly.[80]

G–Use in bullet feeders. "Mr. Bullet Feeder" clearly states that moly coated bullets work very well in their bullet feeder. Their use negates the need of adding mica to hard lubed cast bullets. This is a major advancement especially with CAS. Cowboy shooters use hardcast lead bullets and these are available already lubed with moly.

IMHO: Although used by many shooters, I never liked to use moly bullets because they are messy. Whether you are reloading or just handling cartridges, you get filthy from your fingers to your clothing. I also never needed them because I shot short distances in CAS and USPSA. However there is a new niche for moly bullets–bullet feeders. There is no doubt that increasing sales of both will soon be a reality.

CHAPTER-13

SPECIAL TOPICS

1. Excessive Pressure.

 A–Cause
 B–Signs

2. Reduced Rifle Loads.

 A–H-4895 formula
 B–Other methods
 C–Lead bullets

3. Detonations.

 A–Causes
 B–Prevention
 C–My detonation
 D–Safety features

4. Lead exposure.

 A–Causes
 B–Lead levels
 C–Minimizing exposure

D–Management of high blood levels

E–Symptoms of acute and chronic toxicity

5. Disposal of ammo.

A–Popular suggestions

B–Liability

6. Reloading injuries.

A–Common injuries

B–Indirect mistakes

7. Static electricity.

A–Cause

B–Management

C–Grounding your press

D–Pickup tubes

8. Economics of reloading

1. Excessive Pressure.

Ammo reloading is a well developed art with little need for improvement. In general, follow the manuals and never load above maximum. It seems that powder manufacturers are all pushing their loads away from "lighter" loads because of competition between new high performance powders. This is one of the major reason why reviewing signs of high pressure is so important.[21a]

A–Cause. Assuming you are not loading above maximum, there are situations that will lead to excessive pressures within normal loading ranges. Here a some popular ones:[21a]

- Excessive heat or ammo sitting in the sun
- Using magnum primers when load data lists standard primers, especially if loading at maximum
- Effect on ignition by position sensitive powders
- Cases that are too long may cause the cartridge to get pinched at the end of the chamber
- Sharing loads–a good load for your gun may be catastrophic in some other gun, and vice versa
- Follow published COAL, bullets seated deeper reduces case capacity which will increase pressures.[21a]

B–Signs. Loading a 9mm above industry standard pressures of 35,000 psi, will eventually provide telltale signs of excessive pressure.

This is a list of common signs to look for:[21a]

- Report is louder and recoil is greater than normal
- Difficult extraction caused by residual oil on chamber walls or lube on cases–high pressures will compound the stickiness of the spent round
- Flattening of fired primers is often one of the early signs. As the pressure increases, primers may extrude around the firing pin. Finally the sign of extreme high pressures include a hole in the primer or primers backing out of primer pocket
- Fired primers are falling out of primer pocket
- Case head is expanding and will require full length sizing.[21a]

When these signs are ignored, gun damage or shooter injury may result.

2. Reduced Rifle Loads.

For years hunters have enjoyed using their chosen cartridge and rifle for their chosen game hunt. Now the hunters are aging and reduced loads have been revived–although this is happening at all age levels. This new group is often downsizing the number of guns for other interests, enjoying lower recoil, find the change economical, appreciate less noise, enjoy plinking loads and use them to train youths.[57a]

A–H-4895 formula. There are two kinds of reduced rifle loads:

Somewhat reduced loads. Reduce slow burning powders by 10% of maximum and stay in this range down to minimum load. Some shooters even go below minimum load but should be reminded that slow burning powders with a burn rate of 109(IMR 4350) or slower are hard to ignite and it is not recommended to go below minimum load.[57a]

Really reduced loads using the H-4895 rule. This system is based on extruded single base powders such as H or IMR-4895–the slowest burning propellant that ignites "uniformly" in reduced charges. For every % reduction in the maximum powder charge, the velocity decreases by the same %. The H-4895 rule states that the maximum load can be decreased by 60%.[57a]

As an example, take a H-4895 theoretical load with a minimum of 46 gr. = to a velocity of 2800 fps and a maximum load at 50 gr. = to a velocity of 2900 fps. Multiply 50 gr. by .6 = 30 gr. Note that this 30 gr. load is much lower than the minimum starting load of 46 gr. The new velocity(maximum load 2900 fps multiply by .6) changes to 1740 fps. which is also slower than the minimum starting load of 2800fps.[57b]

There are other slow burning powders that can be used with reduced rifle loads. Compared with H-4895 which has a burn rate of 88/148, they include IMR-3031(79/148), IMR-4198(73/148) and IMR-4227(66/148).[57a]

B–Other methods. There are simple variations and methods that can produce reduced rifle loads and still keep these loads safe.[58]

- Use a small charge of a fast burning powder–for example, 10–12 gr. of Unique with a 165 gr. cast in a 30-06. Flake powders work well with reduced loads because they are easy to ignite. Others include Red Dot and Trail Boss
- Use a shorter case when possible–44 sp. instead of 44 mag.
- Use light weight bullets which produce less recoil
- These reduced rifle loads work best with lead bullets. They are less expensive and require less pressure to push them down the barrel–see section C below.[58]

C–Lead bullets. Reduced loads do not guarantee that the velocity is 1200 fps or less. Check your velocity on a chronograph or manual. More than likely your rifle reduced load will be greater than 1200 fps and you will need to use a gas check to avoid the catastrophe of leading a rifle barrel.

For rifle loads less than 1200 fps, a hardcast lubed bullet with a BH of 18-22 is adequate and more economical. For example, Hunter-Supply has a 165 gr. FP sized .311 for 30-30 tubular magazine priced at $37 for 250 count–large diameter bullets are for extra large bores. Missouri Bullets has a 165 gr. RNFP sized .309 for 30-30 tubular magazine priced at $29 for 250 count plus shipping. Note the difference in bullet diameter to accommodate your rifle bore–most lead 30 caliber rifle bullets are sized .309 which is .001" greater than the jacketed bullets.

The 30 caliber gas checked lubed lead bullets sized .309 are slightly more expensive but are worth it to prevent leading. For example:

Oregon Trail Trueshot 170 gr FN GC sell for $27/100 +shipping.

Gardners Cache 155 gr. FP GC sell for $30/250 +shipping.

Moyer's cast 173 gr. FN GC sell for $44/500 +shipping.

Montana Gold 150 gr. FN GC sell for $23/100 + shipping.

3. Detonations.

A reloading detonation is a situation where a primer fires off during the reloading process. It may be a single primer going off or more likely multiple primers going off in what is called a "daisy chain" or "gang" detonation. This latter one means that when a primer detonates in station 2 of a Dillon XL 650 press, the other primers along the priming wheel can also detonate. When the priming wheel primers detonate, there can be a cascading progression and the magazine tube primers will likely also detonate—a shocking and impressive "WOW-OMG" event!

Gang detonations are the most dreaded of events since as many as 100 primers can be fired at once. This event will damage the priming system and possibly the reloader. Although the Dillon presses have many safety features to protect the operator, it is still prudent to reload with eye and ear protection. **Detonations are rare** but unfortunately are often caused by operator error.

A—Major causes of gang detonations:[6t/4o]

- Number one—operator error
- Slipping the cycling ball or roller handle
- Crushing a primer during priming
- Priming a sideways primer—often caused by a loose and backed out priming arm
- Using soft primers which are more susceptible
- Primers sticking in priming wheel or magazine tube
- Over zealous operator.[6t]
- Forcing a primer into a crimped primer pocket
- Attempting to prime a LPP into a SPP primer pocket
- Forcing a primer onto an unprimed case
- Attempted priming of an off center case/primer pocket
- Decapping upside down primers in station one

- Sparks from static electricity(see section 7 below)
- Forcing the press when there is a problem.[40]

C–Preventive measures. For preventable situations, there are maneuvers that should be avoided or actually be done regularly. Since operator error is the major cause, do not reload if your mind is preoccupied, your reloading session is too long with fatigue resulting or your reloading speed is excessive. Other preventive measures include:[4p]

- Focus on what you are doing–are you loading the correct size primer for the case being reloaded?
- When changing primer size, don't forget to convert the entire priming system
- If you have a static problem in your loading room, ground your press or use anti-cling laundry strips(more in Section 7)
- If a primer does not enter the pocket easily, discard the case
- Do not drop the black plastic rod onto only a few primers in the magazine tube
- Do not tap the black plastic rod onto stuck primers in the magazine or pickup tubes–slowly push them out
- Check range cases for military crimped primer pockets

- Use alcohol to clean the explosive priming compound dust off the RF-100 and loading platform. Clean the magazine and pickup tubes with an alcohol soaked q-tip end. Push this gauze through a large pistol tube with a 22 caliber cleaning rod and use the black plastic rod to push the gauze through a small pistol tube.[4p]

C–My detonation. In 35+ years of reloading, I have had one gang detonation. I had just added oil to the ramming shaft and must have gotten some oil on my cycling hand. I then loaded 100 primers to the magazine tube and resumed reloading. Suddenly the cycling arm/ball came out of my hand at the end of the upstroke and the platform went crashing down unobstructed with a fully loaded magazine tube of primers–WOW-OMG and a few other expletives!

After shaking off the shock, I saw that my entire priming system was destroyed and the black plastic rod had become a rocket that made a large dent in my shed's aluminum roof–but I was not injured despite the soot that accumulated on my face and glasses.

I then made a list of the parts that needed replacement and called Dillon. I told the customer service agent of my gang detonation and the fact that the detonation was certainly "operator error". The agent's first words were "are you OK" followed by "don't bother with your parts list, I am sending you a complete new priming system at no charge".

Despite my insistence that this was a case of operator error, he still refused payment. When the agent was asked if he had any preventive suggestions for the future, he mentioned a possible benefit from using a roller handle instead of the ball type handle. I ordered the roller handle and to this day I feel confident that its use helped me get back into reloading! This roller handle is a major improvement in safety and operational comfort–personal opinion!

C–Safety features. How safe is a reloader from a single or gang detonation? Most presses provide minimal protection from a single detonation. Whether you use a single stage, turret or a progressive press, your face is usually at the same level as the priming process. That is why eye and ear protection is so important even in single detonations. The other issue with single stage and turret presses is the fact that some reloaders use priming tubes of +-50 primers attached to the frame but point at the operator. In case of a single detonation, this primer tube can also turn into a gang detonation that can be pointing at the operator!

Gang detonations that occur in Dillon presses are somewhat directed away from the operator. If you have a detonation that spreads only to the priming wheel, the explosion is somewhat contained by the indexing shellplate. If the explosion spreads to the magazine tube full of primers, the steel pipe covering the primer magazine tube will contain the explosion in the magazine tube/pipe and send its contents upwards into the ceiling.[90]

4. Lead exposure.

Lead exposure can proceed to elevated blood levels which if not corrected can cause acute and chronic toxicity. There are several ways to expose yourself to lead when dealing with lead bullets.

A–The methods that cause elevated blood levels are:[85]

- Reloading. This is the least significant cause. Many shooters buy bulk lead bullets for reloading. In this situation, reloaders have minimal exposure to lead from handling bullets with their finger–since there is minimal absorption through the skin. If necessary, one can always wear gloves.
- Smelting and Casting. Melting wheelweights exposes you to the inhalation of mixed fumes. It should be done outdoors to take advantage of wind to keep fumes away from the operator. Casting also exposes the operator to lead fumes especially if heating lead above 800 degrees F. In both situations, ventilation is the key to protection. As far as handling hot ingots or hot bullets, this should be done with gloved hands–which also requires

special cleaning methods for the contaminated gloves.

- Gun cleaning and case tumbling. Shooters forget that cleaning guns exposes one to lead particles while brushing a barrel or cylinder, as well as wiping the parts with a solvent. The dust generated by your tumbler is also a big source of lead. You should let the tumbler sit several minutes before opening the lid. Then sort the cases/media outside or in a well ventilated area.[85]

- Shooting. During the firing explosion, the lead particulate which is stripped away as the bullet leaves the case and travels down the cylinder and barrel becomes a significant lead exposure. This blowback during the explosion becomes an air blast with a direct hit to the shooter(indoor or outdoor). This is worse in revolvers because of the cylinder/barrel gap.[85]

These four methods of lead exposure raise the blood lead levels through inhalation and ingestion. Avoidance of ingestion via the GI track by "hand to mouth" include: drinking liquids, eating, blowing your nose, wiping your mouth and smoking. Inhalation(aspiration) occurs during normal breathing–obviously worse indoors. There are few inhalation avoidance techniques except wearing a face mask, which is not always feasible.[85]

B–Lead levels. Irrelevant of the source, an elevated blood lead level needs to be addressed before one exhibits toxic manifestations. The typical blood lead level for US adults is less than 10 ug/dl with a mean of 3ug.dl. Nomenclature defined–ug stands for micrograms and dl stands for deciliter. Also 1 ug/dl means 0.01 ppm(parts per million).[85/86]

Any blood level above 10ug/dl is abnormal and potentially dangerous. Of note is that an adult who does not work with lead has a level of 3ug/dl which is the mean mentioned above.[85/86]

C–Minimizing exposure. Lead exposure is cumulative and management always starts with lessening the actual exposure. These are popular examples:[85]

- In competition shooting, it means stay off the firing line except to shoot–do not pick brass, be a spotter or RO
- Wear a mask when cleaning guns and be careful while emptying a tumbler
- When working with lead, do not touch food with your fingers, use a wrapper
- If you smoke do not touch the filter or the filter tip
- Wash hands with regular or lead detergent soap(D-lead wipes or soap) before eating

- Wash shooting clothes often
- Never hesitate to wear nitrile rubber gloves
- Be cautious of indoor ranges. Check for ventilation and lead restrictions.[85]

D–Management of high lead levels. The first step is to remove someone from the known cause. Many high levels will decrease by natural excretion through the kidneys. The therapeutic method of lowering lead levels is by chelation– natural or chemicals.[86]

Some natural products will chelate the lead and assist in its renal excretion. This method has to be monitored by your physician since the chelated lead is still toxic and must be excreted. These natural products include spinurella, chlorella, cilantro and coriander.[86]

- Spinurella is a multi cell and chlorella is a single cell freshwater algae. Both are available at GNC stores in pill form.
- Cilantro is a leaf used in salads, the seed form is called coriander and is used as a cooking spice.[86]

Chemical chelation is a prescribed medication. The oral form of this chelating agent is available. If this is not effective in lowering blood lead levels, then intravenous therapy is indicated.[86]

E–Symptoms of acute and chronic toxicity. Under an

extreme lead exposure, signs of acute poisoning may appear. These include: a metallic taste in your mouth, headache, fatigue, aching peripheral small joints, diarrhea, nausea and abdominal pain.[85]

An unattended blood lead level of 10–25ug/dl will cause lead to start building in the body and will progress to chronic toxicity.[6p] These symptoms include: high blood pressure, chronic fatigue, anemia, mood disorders, memory and concentration deficits, hearing loss, seizures and dementia.[85]

IMHO–Part of removing the exposure may mean changing from lead bullets to plated, coated or jacketed bullets. Moly bullets are lead bullets that are lubed with moly–they still expose you to lead. Depending on your specific exposure, monitoring your blood lead level is the only way to derail the effects of chronic lead poisoning. For more references on the subject, refer to the Cowboy Chronicle, March 2017 issue on page 62.

5. Disposal of ammo.

It is wise to follow the old adage–do not shoot someone else's reloaded ammo and do not give your reloaded ammo to anyone. So what do you do with unwanted ammo? The one thing you must avoid is to place them in the garbage–when the compactor starts things will go "bang". Unfortunately there is no consensus in the forums on the best or accepted method, but here are the popular ones:

- Bury them. Not the best solution but often done by large landowners.
- Disable them with oil or WD-40. This is not durable, the priming compound will eventually dry and be active again.
- Disassemble them and reuse the components. If I am planning to reuse the primers, I use a collet puller or Grip-N-Pull pliers which is non traumatic to the primer. If I am discarding the primers, I use the more aggressive kinetic hammer which can dislodge the primer anvils. If you are reusing the primers, the cases still need to be resized but remove the decapping pin to save the primers in place.[63] Don't be lazy, it is your responsibility to correct a bad reload whether it is a single round or a large batch–dismantling is the only proper solution.

B–Liability. Giving unwanted ammo to a friend is not a wise choice. In face of a catastrophe, your friend will become a litigant and you are totally liable for your reloads. Selling your reloads without a type 6 FFL license is a federal offence. Liability insurance is not affordable for an individual. Incidentally making cast bullets and selling them is also illegal without a type 6 FFL license.[60]

It is obvious that your reloads belong to you and only you can dispose of them properly–dismantle them.

6. Reloading injuries.

Reloading injuries are rare, yet when they occur they are usually the result of a failure in safety rules or operator error. No matter how cautious we are, we all do stupid things. There is a small amount of risk in any activity, especially when working with explosives. Think about what you are doing, stay focused and do not exceed your limits. To reiterate, operator errors do occur because human behavior is prone to mistakes or forgotten safety rules.

A–Common injuries. IMHO, over the years I have accumulated a list of common injuries I have heard about or experienced myself:

- Smashed and lacerated fingers especially when guiding a bullet into the seating die. This should be avoided if you have adequate belling or using a Mr. Bullet Feeder funnel
- Multiple facial or hand injuries from a gang detonation
- Eye injuries or hearing damage from failure to use eye and ear protection–a rare gang detonation is not predictable as well as broken springs that become flying projectiles

B–Cause of direct and indirect injuries. There are situations occurring while reloading which can cause an immediate injury and there are events that can indirectly lead to personal injuries or gun damage while on the firing line. These events are usually the result of operator mistakes. IMHO, these are the common direct ones:

- Decapping flipped primers–use a universal decapping die to slowly push the primer out without tapping it. If you use the sizing die, you will likely end up tapping the anvil and may cause a detonation
- Attempting to reseat a high primer of a loaded round–the most dangerous move in reloading! Change to softer primers!
- Transferring a bin full of ammo into your holding container–do it slowly and in close proximity to the receiving container
- Forcing primers into tight primer pockets

These are the indirect ones:[62]

- Failure of proper case inspection–split cases can rupture during firing
- Cases dented by excessive lube can lead to premature metal failure
- Loading an accidental double charge or a squib
- Loading rifle cases exceeding maximum COAL
- Seating bullets too far out

- Producing excessively crimped rounds
- Taking the wrong powder when filling or refilling the powder hopper–have only one powder on the loading bench
- Emptying the powder hopper into the wrong powder container–always check before pouring.[62]

IMHO, my worse fear in reloading was to produce a squib or double charge. This was resolved years ago when I purchased a powder check for my XL 650. It is wise for all reloaders to use a powder check or lock out die–especially so if you do not use an auto indexing press.

7. Static electricity.

Static electricity is an imbalance of electric charges within or on the surface of a material. The charge remains until it is able to move away by means of an electric current or electrical discharge. It is this discharge that is a nuisance and or danger to reloaders–as a small spark can ignite priming dust and other explosive mixtures.[75]

A–Cause. There are several well known basic causes:[75]

- Dry air with humidity less than 40%
- Cold dry air brought in a warm building
- Rugs(especially wool or nylon) cause friction which tends to charge personnel

- Electrical resistance in shoes–wool or nylon compared to rubber or leather shoes
- Shuffling gain increases friction
- Other flooring. Concrete or wood are ideal, whereas synthetic tiles, polymer rugs and laminate are a problem
- Operator clothing. Wool is bad and cotton is good.[75]

B–Management. It is geared toward the prevention of this issue.

- Spray rugs and furniture with anti static coatings
- Wear an #3 anti static brush tied to your wrist(available on Amazon)
- De-charge your body by touching a grounded object before touching your press
- Increase humidity with a humidifier or use an air ionizer
- Add a rubber floor mat next to your press
- The ultimate solution is to ground your press.[75]

C–Grounding your press. This process can easily be done if you know basics in electricity, can use a multi-meter and can prove that the press is grounded. I have grounded my own press but since I am not an electrician, I am liable if I describe the simple process and something goes wrong.

What I suggest is that you prepare your press by scraping

the paint off the metal and clamping a copper wire to the base metal. The other end needs to be attached to a proven ground by an electrician. For those of you who feel comfortable in attempting this simple task, I refer you to four good references on the process–# 91–94.

D–Pickup tubes. It is not enough to clean the loading platform and priming wheel with alcohol. You also need to clean the pickup tubes and magazine tube. I have already mentioned their cleaning with alcohol but will now review a method with dish soap/water. Soak the tubes in a dish full of a regular mixture of soap and water and let them drip dry. The soap film left in the tubes prevents static electricity.[75]

The purpose of cleaning tubes is to remove the priming compound that appears as dust. The biggest source of this dust comes from the use of a RF-100 primer loader. The vibration caused by this machine is a great source of loose dust that gets transferred to the RF-100 collecting tube, then transferred to the magazine tube and finally to the priming wheel.[75]

8. Economics of reloading.

Some shooters buy their ammo and occasionally shoot at the range. Others like to load a batch for their next visit to the range. The real shooter loads a large supply of ammo and then can go to the range at will and shoot freely to their heart's content. Which category do you fall in?

The current argument against reloading is that there are no longer enough savings to make reloading worthwhile. This may be true if you are one of these "batch" reloaders who buy one pound of powder, 1500 primers and bullets at a local gun shop. These reloaders end up paying top price for a year's supply of pistol ammo.

The practical reloader will buy an 8 pound jug of powder, ten+ thousand primers and bulk bullets in the thousands. For this kind of order, they look for sales, waived hazardous fees, free shipping, lost leaders, bulk sales and sales of the week. For these mega orders, they buy from internet retailers. The key is to shop around and even try web suppliers that may not be your usual providers. Sometimes you have to take your second choice in components especially when there seems to be a shortage of powder and primers. When you find deals, buy even if there is not an immediate need–stock up but do not hoard.

I recently did the reloading math for 9mm and 38 special. I found that with my bulk components, I can load 1000 rounds of each for $125–this is about half the price of loaded ammo. Reloading can also be a labor of love and a hobby. Consequently if you need large amounts of ammo for competition, practice or pleasure shooting, reloading is the only economical way to shoot freely.

CHAPTER-14

FAQ'S

When you write a book which includes extensive research, you find many useful tips. Each of these tips are useable items for all reloaders. Yet these short subjects do not fill a chapter or even a page since most can be answered within a single paragraph or less.

Most FAQ's have a reference at the end of the answer, if there is no reference it is an answer IMHO. Some of the FAQ's relate to shooting and many apply to the use of a Dillon XL 650 press.

1. What to do when the plunk test fails–how to identify the problem?[6u]

> Paint the failed round with a black marker to cover the bullet and case. Drop it into the barrel or cartridge gage and rotate it back and forth. The results and solutions are:
>
> • Scratches on a bullet–COAL is too long
> • Scratches on the edge of the case mouth–insufficient crimp

- Scratches just below the case mouth–too much crimp
- Scratches on the case just below the bullet–bullet seated crooked from inadequate belling
- Scratches on the case just above the extractor groove–the case bulge was not removed with sizing. May need to lower the sizing die or use a push through sizing die.[6u]

2. Why does the case bell adjustment not hold?[1h]

The securing nut that holds the powder die in the toolhead is getting loose and the powder die is moving up, especially if the collar clamp screws of the powder measure are not tight.[1h]

3. Why are primers backing out on firing?[8g]

Primer pockets enlarge after many firings. Eventually the wide primer pockets will not hold primers. Also very light loads will cause primers to back out during firing and stay out. This is not a crucial issue with auto pistols but it will lock up a revolver.[8g]

4. Is there one powder that can be used in all pistol loads?[8h]

> Unique has historically been a popular powder to reload all pistol cartridges. Clays is also favorably mentioned.[8h] IMHO, Titegroup has potential for filling this niche.

5. What is the proper way of draining powder from the hopper?[4q]

> Remove the failsafe rod and you have two choices. Pull the entire tool head off the press and pour out the powder. The other method is to remove the powder measure from the toolhead by loosening the two collar clamp screws.[4q]

6. Why is my powder measure malfunctioning after dumping powder?[6v]

> When you remove the powder measure off the toolhead, be careful not to loose the white delrin sleeve inside the connector body—if it falls out you will likely find it on the bench or inside the powder container.[6v]

7. Why do my cases get hung up on the ejector wire?[1i]

> The ejector wire needs lubrication. Spray Hot Shot case lube on the wire and shellplate slots that hold the cases. The ejector wire can bind the cases especially

if you have updated to a shellplate bearing kit. There must not be a gap between the wire and the shellplate. This requires bending the wire in the angle as it enters the hole in the platform and often bending the wire outwards toward station 5. There are detailed steps in the bearing kit instruction sheet on how to properly bend the ejector wire.[1i]

The most common cause for breaking the index ring is a cartridge that doesn't eject cleanly because of binding on the ejector wire. This puts and overload on the indexer and the wire needs proper bending. This requires bending the wire as mentioned above.[10f]

8. Why do my primers have a dent in them?[9p]

Primer dents are a cosmetic problem. Pressure dents do not fire primers, they need a striking pressure to detonate. Debris or powder falls on the priming punch and the punch simply needs wiping. In a new machine the primer punch is "turned out" and occasionally this leaves a tiny button on the face–it needs to be ground off.[9p]

9. Why is my powder check drawing powder out of the case?[10g]

The solutions are varied–use the one that works.

- Polish the brass end that enters the case.

- Clean the rod and brass end with alcohol.
- Rub graphite on the rod and brass end.
- Rub the rod and brass end with a laundry static sheet.[10g]

10. Why is my press clogging up at the top of the casefeeder tube?[10h]

This is caused by a jiggling casefeeder. Secure the casefeeder to the wall or ceiling.[10h]

11. My shellplate is out of time–what to do?[10i]

Call Dillon. They will send you a free alignment tool #13713 with detailed and easy instructions. If you need some help, call Dillon again once the alignment tool arrives–if you are near your press they will walk you through the process.[10i]

12. Why are my cases not completely entering station 1 shellplate slot?[1j]

The weak link in the XL 650 press is the casefeed slide(black triangular block). Assuming you have been greasing the face of the block, they still wear out a channel and need replacement. The worst spot is the screw that holds the top portion of the slide to its base–it eventually strips in the plastic and keeps loosening which causes the problem.[1j]

Another common cause is the casefeed slide spring. It often weakens or breaks and needs replacement.

13. How do I adjust the primer seating depth?[1k]

> There are no adjustments in primer seating depth. Priming has a hard stop with the XL 650. Primers are always seated .001" below flush and if using soft primers or different brands can be as low as .007".[1k] When priming, set the primer on the primer pocket base by utilizing the hard stop to guarantee proper ignition.

14. What is cerrosafe?[59a/b]

> This is a gunsmith's tool for measuring gun chambers and removing broken case necks from forcing cones/barrels as well as any stuck case parts. It is an alloy of bismuth, lead, cadmium and indium. It costs $15 for a ½ pound bar and it is reusable. It melts a 158–190° F. and exhibits the quality of shrinking slightly during initial cooling to assist in extracting metal from the firearms. About 1 hour after cooling it expands to the original size to allow measuring of the chambers.[59a/b]

15. Why do I have inconsistent charges?[1L]

The case pushing on the powder funnel is what activates the powder bar to travel its full length. With range cases you have some cases that are shorter in length than others, these cases will not activate the powder bar to travel its total distance—yielding a lower charge.[1L]

16. Why do I get primers seating sideways?[1m/1n]

- Excessive loading speed
- Anchor press properly to a stable fixed bench to prevent shaking and jiggling. The casefeeder also needs to be anchored as mentioned in #10
- Clean the bottom and top of the priming wheel. A dirty and sticky wheel will certainly turn primers
- Make sure the priming seating punch is threaded tightly. If it backs out the primers will start flipping.[1m]
- Shellplate is too springy. Tighten the bolt or install a shellplate bearing kit
- CCI primers are more likely to go sideways because of the taper shape of the cup
- Of note—upside down primers are usually caused by the RF-100 filling machine, not the reloading press.[1n]

17. What are causes of broken indexer rings?[4r]

- Shellplate bolt is too tight
- Primer seating punch is sticking in the upward position
- Deformed case rim preventing ejection at station 5
- Lack of proper lubrication with synthetic grease to ring and indexer block. Using oil on this part will lead to earlier failure since oil softens plastic parts

18. How do I clear my pickup tubes of stuck primers?[1o]

If primers don't fall out of pickup tube, do not push them through into the magazine tube since the same problem will occur in the presses's magazine tube. You need to perform a "reverse drain" on the pickup tube–for SP use the plastic rod and gently "push" on the anvil side of the primers. Never tap on the primers, even on the anvil side. This technique can be done with better protection by pushing on the primers with the pickup tube inside a ½ inch steel pipe.[1o] For LP tubes, use a 22 cal. cleaning rod to push the primer.

After clearing the tube, determine if the tube is scratched. Drop a new single primer in the tube, if it hangs up the tube is scratched and should be discarded. If you wish to check the remaining primers of this batch, drop each one through a good tube and discard any that hang up. If you cannot clear a tube using reasonable force, then discard the tube.[1o]

19. Do I need carbide sizing dies for pistols?[1p]

Carbide dies need less lube and use less force to process. The big difference is in durability. Standard sizing dies last +-52,000 loads whereas carbide sizing dies last 750,000 loads. A volume reloader would quickly use up a standard die.[1p]

20. Why do I get crushed primers?[1q]

There are three common causes. First is the old problem of trying to prime a crimped primer pocket. Second is a shellplate out of time as previously noted in # 11. Third is a need for adjustment of station 2 locator tab, the arm should be .002-.005" away from touching the case(use a feeler gage to adjust).[1q]

21. Why is my shellplate indexing sluggishly?[1r]

- Shellplate bolt is too tight–this will break the indexer ring
- Lack of grease under the shellplate bolt
- Rotating ring and block indexer need grease

- A rubbing ejector wire on the shellplate can slow it down. Keep a narrow gap between the two. If it is touching, lube the wire with One Shot.[1r]

22. How much can I load my casefeeder hopper?[1s]

A blue cartridge bin will hold 250-350 count 38 special cases or 300-400 count 9mm cases and this appears to be a good amount that works well. If the plate moves slowly from overloading, it is hard on the motor and may lead to a premature major failure.[1s]

If the two set screws under the plate are loose, the clutch will slip and the plate will be sluggish or stop turning. The goal is to set the clutch screws to handle an appropriate load without slipping.[1s]

23. Why is powder spilling from the powder funnel?[1t]

Powder measure is not closing completely with the handle all the way forward. Tighten the blue wing nut–holding the handle forward, the rod spring should be 75% compressed. The other common cause is powder sticking in the drop tube secondary to static electricity. Remove the drop tube and wipe it inside and out with an anti-static laundry strip.[1t]

24. Why is my powder hopper changing colors?[1u]

> Powder left in the hopper will make the clear plastic discolor. Some powders such as Titegroup are more likely to discolor. When the hopper becomes opaque, Dillon will replace it. The older models had a hopper glued to the metal frame. Remove it and drill the metal frame to hold two screws to secure the new one.[1u]

25. How do I change my indexer ring?[1v]

> Remove the shellplate, primer assembly and entire platform. Change the ring per instructions. Reassemble the parts by using the platform and shellplate realignment tools from Dillon. If you don't have these tools, you have to eyeball the primer punch alignment.[1v]

26. Why do I get a light primer strike and misfire?[10j]

> This is usually caused by a high primer. The first strike only seats the primer, the second will fire.[10j]

27. Is there a hand held depriming tool?[10k]

> The "Harvey deprimer"($50) is a hand held depriming tool that deprimes all major cases without the use of dies, shellholders or presses. It is available through harveydeprimer.com.[10k]

28. Why do Dillon replacement plastic parts come in changing colors?[4s]

> Whenever Dillon changes a part for improved function and reliability, the parts change color. For example, the ring indexer has gone from black to yellow and now grey.[4s]

29. Should I use the long spring on the powder measure?[4t]

> Use this spring. It smooths the bar return instead of the jolt without it.[4t]

30. Why should I not reload self defense ammo?

> IMHO and according to many forums, reloading self defense ammo is not wise. It is a way for lawyers to point out that the reloads were loaded hotter than commercial ammo—it may carry a wrong intent to do more harm!

31. Why use an "on off" timer on my tumbler?

> IMHO, this is a cheap item that will save a batch of cases. Set the timer and walk away. Without the timer, we have all forgotten a running tumbler overnight or longer—causing a thinning of the metal which will make the cases start splitting prematurely.

32. What should I disregard when reading shooting forums?

IMHO, do not use individual favorite load data, always refer to your manual. Be leary of single discussant personal opinions.

33. What are causes of "blown cases"?[14c]

- Excessive pressure caused by a bullet setback–usually secondary to an inadequate taper crimp in auto pistols or a roll crimp in a revolver. Use the bench press test to check for bullet setback–press a loaded cartridge against a fixed bench, if the bullet sets back the crimp is inadequate
- Weak cases from repeated reloading
- Excessive crimping in auto pistols can cause the case mouth to jam into the barrel throat instead of headspacing on the case mouth. This will lead to excessive pressures
- Loading above maximum load. If a case is rated 20,000 psi at maximum load, loading it to 25-27,000 will likely blow the case.[14c]

34. Why are self defense loads labeled +P?[60]

This ammo has been commercially loaded to higher pressures than standard maximum loads. This is done to add enough energy to reliably deliver an expanded bullet deep enough to be effective in self defense.[60]

35. What do SAAMI specs stand for?[61]

(Sporting Arms and Ammunition Manufacturer's Institute). They dictate everything from the cartridge dimensions to the maximum pressure that a cartridge should produce. Gun manufacturers use their specs to build their barrels and chambers to contain a maximum load. They also test firearms with a "proof load"–a high pressure load much higher than a maximum load, to replicate a worse case scenario.[61]

36. This final section covers quick tips that I have accumulated over the years and are all IMHO:

- SWC bullets are impossible bullets to disassemble with a collet puller or Grip-N-Pull pliers–use a kinetic hammer
- Walnut media lasts longer than corn because the kernel edges stay sharp since walnut is harder than corn
- The easy way to see the content of your casefeeder hopper is to place a mirror on the ceiling
- The Dillon powder cap is not a tight seal. Powder left in the hopper can absorb moisture

or dehydrate–either way it will falsely change the weight of your charge

- When a bullet falls in a case after sizing, the case walls are too thin to properly hold a crimp–they should be discarded

- Lyman Tuff Nut media has "rouge" added as a polishing agent. RCBS has corn media with their own case lube added

- When starting a reloading session, the Dillon powder measure needs 8-10 rounds for the powder to settle under the baffle–then you start producing reproducible charge weights

- Dillon stuck case remover is a built in feature in their rifle sizing dies. For instructions, go to you tube and search "Removing stuck rifle case on a Dillon full length sizing die"

- The practical reloader uses Lyman, LEE, RCBS, Hornady and Dillon. The benchrest shooter uses higher precision products from Redding, Sinclair, Foster and many more

- Use a deep well socket to tighten dies instead of a wrench that doesn't always fit properly on the nut

- Primer drawback is when decapped primers stick on the decapping pin and are drawn back in the primer pocket. The solution is filing and rounding off the end of the decapping pin. This is less of a problem with Dillon dies since the decapping pin is spring loaded which pushes the primer off

- For a loosening wing nut on the fail safe rod, add a lock nut with a plastic insert

- When removing the fail safe rod to empty the powder hopper, the white Delrin bushing needs to be popped downward and replaced the same way. Any horizontal push or pull through the metal teeth will result in splitting the bushing

- Station 1 rarely gets an inverted case that won't size and occasionally has a failed decapping so don't force priming in station 2 if the new primer will not enter the pocket easily

- Always label your ammo containers with caliber, bullet weight, powder type/weight, type of primer and date of reloading

- When reloading a new load, it is wise to check this load out at the range before loading hundreds of rounds–the best advice in preventing unwanted ammo.

Summary

RELOADING–A PRACTICAL HOBBY

Reloading is not a "necessary evil". If you belong to one or more shooting sports, you will need to develop a system for supplying the fodder you need to support these sports. The best of all worlds is to convert your reloading sessions into a "practical hobby". If you like to shoot and reload, then you have a double passtime.

This book leaned heavily on the use of Dillon equipment. These chapters included the Dillon XL 650, the Square Deal B and its accessories and upgrades. The Square Deal B is probably the most economical progressive press that is trouble free–especially for beginners. The Dillon XL 650 is an engineering marvel and the ultimate progressive reloader–IMHO.

There is a long chapter on other reloading presses and accessory equipment by Lee, Lyman, Hornady and RCBS. I hope that the chapter on MY shooting history, shooting sessions and casting years were not overbearing. I included these to give some credibility to my credentials as an experienced shooter, reloader and casting master. It was not done to berate others–it was meant to show how I do it "my way". I encourage my readers to vary "my way" to fit their specific needs. There were many other chapters that supported my method and many chapters on new material–such as new powders and new bullets.

"Special topics" included material that was based on theory, general knowledge and opinions of multiple forums. The forums provided old and accepted "tried and true" ideas as well as the modern approaches to change. I have heavily footnoted and referenced my sources to give appropriate credit. The references give the reader an opportunity to refer to the sources–to read the entire articles and forums.

In conclusion, I wrote about what I like and know– RELOADING. It provides creativity, gratification in producing quality ammo and can become a long term HOBBY. Everyday I see reloaders exhibiting PRIDE in their work–I hope that this personal satisfaction extends to my readers.

Abbreviations

ac	Auto Comp powder
bb	bevel base
bc	ballistic coefficient
berb	Berry bullets
bh	brinell hardness
bt	boat tail
cn	conical nose
COAL	cartridge over all length
CFE	copper fouling eraser
CMJ	complete metal jacket
cup	copper units of pressure
dcl	Dillon case lube
dia.	diameter
DS	double struck or sized twice
FAQ's	frequently asked questions
fb	flat base
fed	federal brass
fls	full length sizing
fmj	full metal jacket
fn	flat nose
fps	feet per second
Ftx	flex tip bullet
FYI	for your information

GC	gas check
gr.	grain
hb	hollow base
hc	hard cast
HS	headstamp
hp	hollow point bullet
jsp	jacketed soft spoint
id	internal diameter
IMHO	in my honest opinion
jff	just for fun
LMP	large magnum primers
LPP	large pistol primers
LRP	large rifle primers
lrn	lead round nose
lswc	lead semi wadcutter
MBF	Mr. Bullet Feeder
Moly	molybdenum disulfide lube
NRV	new ruger vaquero
oal	overall length(same as COAL)
+P	extra pressure and velocity
PMC	PMC brand of brass
PF	Power factor
PP	Power Pistol powder
psi	pounds per square inch
RAP	Ruger American Pistol
rn	round nose

RRL	reduced rifle loads
S & B	Sellier and Belliot
SDB	Square Deal B
SMP	small magnum primer
SPP	small pistol primer
SP	standard plate in plated bullets
SRP	small rifle primer
sst	super shock tip bullet
swc	semi wadcutter
TMJ	total metal jacket(same as complete metal jacket)
TP	thick plate(plated bullets)
xtp	extreme terminal performance bullets
zerk	grease fitting

Footnotes–References

Group 1 Footnotes dillonprecision.com/forum

Equipment section–XL 650

1a	Blue Press specs and prices
1b	Dillon reloading accessories
1c	Dillon XL 650 manual–Version 6.1
1d	"Split casefeed insert slide" 11/13/10
1e	"A couple of XL 650 issues"
1f	dillonupgrades.com/XL 650
1g	"Primer seating adjustments on 650" 9/15/15
1h	"Case flare loss" 12//29/16
1i	"Ejector wire" 12/20/09
1j	"XL casefeed issues" 10/22/12
1k	"Deep set primers" 12/6/15
1l	"Inconsistent powder charge" 11/15/15
1m	"Primers seating sideways" 4/5/08
1n	"Sideway primers" 8/6/13
1o	"Primers getting stuck in pickup tube" 3/3/15
1p	"Carbide or standard dies" 3/14/15
1q	"Crushed primers" 8/31/14
1r	"Problem at the start–sluggish shellplate" 8/21/14
1s	"Casefeeder capacity" 8/30/13

1t   "Powder spilling from funnel" 8/19/13

1u   "Powder hopper changing colors" 7/19/16

1v   "Broke my 650 indexing ring" 2/15/15

Group 2 Footnotes dillonprecision.com/forum

Other Dillon equipment section

2a   "Shellplate bearing kit" 12/11/13

2b   "Why tumble cases" 11/28/11

2c   Dillon rotary tumblers/ultrasonic cleaners

2d   Dillon rapid polish 290

2e   Dillon depriming prior to tumbling

2f   Dillon rotary case/media separators

2g   Dillon brass collectors/sorters

2h   "Tip for scale" 9/10/16

2i   Dillon electronic scales

2j   Dillon rapid trim 1500(RT1500)

2k   CED millennium 2 Chronograph

2l   Dillon case lube

2m   "One shot case lube and powder sticking" 11/6/16

2n   "Removal of case lube" 2/12/13
      "Removing case lube" 11/21/10
      dillonprecision.com/removing-case-lube

2o   "Stuck cases in sizing/decapping die" 12/26/16

2p   "9mm cartridge gauge" 12/24/16

2q   Dillon general info of RF-100

2r   "RF-100 flipping primers" 4/25/10

Group 3 Footnotes dillonprecision.com/forum

Equipment section—Square Deal B

3a   Blue Press specs and prices

3b   SDB 2009 Manual

3c   Lubrication—you tube video "Lubricating the dillon precision square deal B" 9/11/15

3d   FAQ'S by Dillon, dillonprecision.com/forum

  3d1   "Primer slide not always loading" 5/6/13

  3d2   "Multiple primers falling out" 2/11/13

  3d3   "Primers falling out" 11/3/11

  3d4   "cci primers" 5/18/08

  3d5   "Persistent problems with primer system" 11/15/16

  3d6   "Priming issue" 6/20/10

  3d7   "Toolhead friction plate" 10/30/12

  3d8   "Rounds wont fit case gage" 4/16/10

  3d9   "Swelling cases" 6/9/10

  3d10   "Stuck brass" 5/4/13

  3d11   "Auto indexing trouble" 12/28/10

  3d12   "Resizing die picking up brass" 11/23/12

  3d13   "Shellplate rotates counterclockwise" 4/9/10

  3d14   "Flipped primers" 6/22/14

Group 4 Footnotes forums.brianenos.com

General reloading–Brian Enos's Forums...Maku Mozo

Reloading section–Dillon precision reloading

4n   "Brass sticking to powder drop tube" 12/27/15

4o   "Primer detonations" 11/21/16

4p   "Large primers sticking" 2/1/13

4q   "Removing powder from the 650 hopper properly" 11/7/16

4r   "Ring indexer" 1/16/16

4s   "Dillon FAQ's–plastic parts changing colors"

4t   "Dillon FAQ's–long spring on 650 powder measure"

Group 5 Footnotes forums.brianenos.com

General reloading–Brian Enos's Forums...Maku Mozo

Reloading section–non Dillon reloading equipment

5a   "Volume decision for buying/single/turret/progressive" 1/1/15

5b   "Single stage for bullet puller" 10/23/16

5c   "When should you use an undersize sizing die" 10/17/16

5d   "How to measure primer depth" 3/19/16

Group 6 Footnotes forums.brianenos.com

General reloading–Brian Enos's Forums...Maku Mozo

Reloading section–general reloading

6a   "Blowing up a gun" 3/29/15

6b   "What can you do with a single stage press" 1/17/17

Group 7 Footnotes forums.brianenos.com

General reloading–BrianEnos's forums...Maku Mozo

Reloading section–9mm/38 caliber

7a   "Slide will not fully close when cycling" 8/4/16

7b   "Magnum primers in 9mm" 1/18/16

7c   "What causes fliers" 2/3/16

7d   "Major or Minor" 3/21/12

7e   "9mm minor load data" 11/19/16

7f   "CFE Pistol 9mm major–first go" 5/8/14

7g   "Winchester auto comp" 11/3/11

7h   "Hi–tek bullets" 6/30/16

7i   "Coating bullets" 12/10/16

7j   "Plated or coated" 11/23/16

Group 8 Footnotes forumsbrianenos.com

General Reloading–Brian Enos's forums...Maku Mozo

Reloading section–44/45 caliber

8a   "Bulge below bullet in case" 10/2/14

8b   "Small rifle primers with small pocket 45acp brass" 4/13/15

8c   "Reloading 44 magnum" 11/14/12

8d   "Using small pistol primers in 45acp brass" 8/31/15

8e   "45acp small vs. large primers" 1/11/16

8f   "45acp shaving coating when seating" 5/11/15

8g   "Having trouble with primers backing out" 10/5/15

8h   "Univ./unique" 1/8/17

      re: One powder for all pistols.

Group 9 Footnotes dillonprecision.com/forum

General reloading–Rifle and handgun calibers

9a   "Dillon dies vs. small base dies" 5/3/16

9b   "Carbide dies" 11/5/16

9c   "Slight ridge in 45acp with auto/tapered cases" 1/23/13

9d   "dillonprecision.com/proper amount of bell(9mm)" 4/16/16

9e   "Case expansion result on 9mm" 12/11/16

9f   "357 magnum issues" 12/8/13

      re: powder not falling

9g   "Extruded powder blues" 5/8/09

9i   "Powder spillage" 12/1/16

9j   "Powder dumping on shellplate" 2/7/11

9k   "Dillon 650 unique tek Whidden clamped toolhead" 1/26/16

9l   "Loading small primers" 5/9/13

9m   "45acp with small primers" 11/9/12

9n   "Cast bullets in glock pistols" 2/10/11

9o   "Primer explosion" 8/23/09

9p   "Seated primers with dents" 8/14/13

Group 10 Footnotes forums.brianenos.com

General reloading–Brian Enos's forums...Maku Mozo

Reloading section–FAQ's

10a   "9mm cases settling under casefeed plate" 5/17/15

10b   "Ammo will not chamber" 8/14/08

10c   "9mm cases" Handloadersbench.com 6/16/16

10d   "Bullets seating crooked" 1/9/16

10e   "9mm problems" 8/21/14 handloadersbench.com
      "Magnum small pistol vs. small pistol primers in 9mm"
      2/6/11

10f   "Breaking the indexer ring" in Tips and Tricks

10g   "XL 650 powder check drawing powder out of case"
      2/23/15

10h   "Why is my press clogging up at top of XL 650 feeder
      tube" in Tips and Tricks

10i   "Shellplate timing issues" In Tips and Tricks

10j   "A light strike" In Tips and Tricks

10k   "Handheld depriming tool" in harveyprimer.com

Group 11 Footnotes thefiringline.com

Handloading, reloading, and bullet casting section

11a   "Found another bonus with Dillon powder check die"
      1/5/17

11b   "Hornady brass issue" 11/29/10

11c   "Primer pocket uniforming options" 11/21/16

11d   "Ammo reloading" 12/22/16

11e   "Powder drop accuracy" 12/9/12

11f   "XL 650 primers not feeding" 1/20/17

11g   "Alliant power pistol" 12/27/08 and 11/20/14

11h   "A compensator....what does it do" 12/16/10

11i   "Sizing powder coated bullets" 12/21/14

Group 12 Footnotes thefirearmsforum.com

Ammo and reloading section

12a   "Progressive presses" 8/16/16

12b   "I screwed up and need honest advice" 1/2/17

12c   "Rotary vs. vibrating" LD Bennett 9/15/09

12d   "Trimming rifle cases" LD Bennett 3/18/10

12e   "Stuck cases" 12/16/16

12f   "Explaining headspace" 6/6/10

12g   "Questions about sizing rifle brass–necking down"
      10/25/16 by LD Bennett

12h   "Questions about sizing rifle......same as 12g

12i   "Advanced reloading techniques" LD Bennett 3/18/10

12j   "Neck sizing" "partial sizing" LD Bennett/Glen Moulton 1/1/17

12k   "Crimping" LD Bennett 3/18/10

12l   "30-30 crimp" Lee factory crimp

12m   "Primers not consistent" LD Bennett 12/31/16

12n   "About manuals" LD Bennett 3/18/10

Group 13 Footnotes reloadersnest.com/forum

General Reloading

13a   "Lyman No 55 powder measure trial and error system—how to set it" 3/17/16

13b   "Balance beam or digital powder scale" 4/11/10

13c   "Dies" 10/21/16

Group 14 Footnotes handloadersbench.com

metallic cartridge reloading

handgun cartridge

14a   "9mm and oal" 1/2/17

14b   "Antiquated technology" 2/22/14

14c   "Blown case" 1/8/17

Group 15 Footnotes handloadersbench.com

metallic cartridge reloading

Reloading for rifles

15a   "Case dent" 11/30/16
15b   "Diagnosing stuck cases" 12/27/16
15c   "Small pistol primers vs. small pistol magnum primers" 6/3/16

Group 16 Footnotes

thehighroad.org/index.ph?/forums

Handloading and Reloading

16a   "Bean vs. electronic scales" 1/24/15
16b   "Thinking about trying plated bullets" 11/7/12
16c   "Polygonal barrels and rainier bullets/berry's" 3/7/12

Group 17 Footnotes

Hornady handbook of cartridge reloading–9th edition

17a   Introduction to calibers
17b   Load data

Group 18 Footnotes

Hodgdon on line hodgdonreloading.com

18a   Reloading data center or annual manual 2017

18b   Trail Boss reduced loads

18c   Load data–Berry bullets

Group 19 Footnotes

Speer reloading manual #12

19a   Intro to each caliber

19b   Load data

19c   Taper crimping for semi auto pistols. pp 429–432.

19d   9mm choice of powders(9mm intro section page 498)

Group 20 Footnotes handloadermagazine.com

20   Reduced loads

Group 21 Footnotes

Lee modern reloading 2nd edition

21a   Chapter 8 pp108–115 All about pressure

21b   Powder measure improved kit of dippers.

22a   "RCBS lock out die–part 1: theory of operation" 9/19/10 ultimatereloader.com

23a   "RCBS lock out die" 3/21/12
smith-wessonforum.com/reloading

24   midwayusa.com On line catalog

25   Group 25 Footnotes–youtube.com

25a   youtube.com "Lubrication of the Dillon precision XL650" 9/11/15

25b   youtube.com "Cleaning the Dillon precision square deal B" 9/11/15

25c   youtube.com "Handle hard to push/pull" 2/21/15

26   uniquetek.com/product

26a   Convert XL 650 to single stage

26b   XL 650 upgrades

26c   Primer tube stand

26d   Floating die toolhead #T1384 re: Whidden Gunworks toolhead

27   RCBS Reloading Master Catalog 2016

28   Hornady 2017 master catalog

28a   Products

28b   One shot case lube

28c   Cowboy seating die

28d   Match grade dies

28e   Power pistol–Hornady manual 9th edition Page 769

28f   Bullets–Interlock, Flex tip and XTP

29   inlinefabrication.com

29a   Light system–LED kit

29b   XL 650 Sky Light

29c   Primer tube stand

30   ebay.com Spent primer upgrade fix on Square Deal B

31   mr.bulletfeeder.com

32   softec.it.com/di/ex/digas

33   brasstumbler.com/articles/how–long

34a   "Digital scales vs. balance beam" 11/22/12
      shootersforum.com/handloading equipment

35a   "Reloading scales, your ammo's accuracy hangs in the
      balance" By Phelps Marsaro 5/14/14

36   ch4d.com "A single stage press–swager

37   forums.brianenos.com Chronograph equipment section

37a   "How necessary is a chronograph" 8/14/15

38   egwguns.com U die

39   Per manuals Lee 2nd Edition, Hodgdon 2017, Hornady
      9th edition, Speer #12

40   "The Ruger American Pistol" 12/29/15
      americanrifleman.org

41   "American pistol" Ruger–firearms.com

42   bluesheepdog.com/2016/08/22/ruger–american
      –manual–safety

43   thefirearmsblog.com/blog/2016/08/find–safety

44   "Gun review: Ruger American Pistol" 1/5/16
      thetruthaboutguns.com

45   REVIEWS rugerforum.net/ruger/pistol
      · neg "Shot the Ruger American pistol 9mm"
         12/31/16

- pos "Ruger American 45acp" 11/23/16
- pos "RAP sear block" 12/20/16
- neg "Questions to those with RAP with manual safety" 12/14/16
- neg "FYI to those looking to install sights on the RAP" 11/15/16
- pos "Ruger American conclusion" 10/27/16

46   alliantpowder.com

47   "A fast look at Hodgdon's CFE Pistol powder" 8/6/14 in shootingtimes.com

48   Winchesterguns.com

49   "Winchester auto comp ball powder" 3/15/10 by tannerbrass.com/winchester-autocomp

50   **IMRpowder.com/pdf/trailboss**

50a   **Trail Boss**

50b   **How to determine min. and max loads of TB**

51   **castboolits.gunloads.com**

51a   **"Trailboss powder" 6/25/12**

51b   **"Do bullets metal from firing" 6/4/13**

52   "What are the different types of bullets and what do they do" in thetruthaboutguns.com 7/18/13

53   berrybullets.com

54   cbbullets.com re: hard cast bullets

55   "What is the HI-TEK coating and how is it applied" in missouribullet.com FAQ's

56   sncasting. com

57a   "Reduced rifle loads" by John Barsness Feb 2017
      in handloadermagazine.com Somewhat/really reduced
      loads

57b   "Hodgdon H–4895 reduced rifle loads" H–4895 60%
      formula in hodgdon.com

58   "5 ways I make reduced ammunition loads" 5/11/16
      in ammoland.com

59   What is cerrosafe

59a   brownells.com/guntech/cerrosafe

**59d   gunsmithtalk.wordpress.com/what-is-cerrosafe
      2/25/11**

60   "Concealed carry: what about + p ammo" 11/7/13
      in dailycaller.com

61   "Ask foghorn: what does +p and +p+ mean" 7/22/13
      in SAAMI.org and thetruthaboutguns.com

62   Add to 6-q shootingtimes.com/reloading/10–common
      12/3/14

63   Add to 6-o luckygunner.com/lounge/safely–dispose
      "How to safely dispose of bad ammo" 10/2/14

64   thefirearmsforum.com "9mm reloading issues" 8/4/12

65   smith–wessonforum.com "problems with clays in
      9mm" 3/12/10

66   thehighroad.com
      "9mm brass–is there a significant difference" 1/19/15

67 thefirearmsforum.com "9mm recipes for plated bullets" 9/9/13

68 thehighroad.org "reloading die comparision" 10/21/12

69 thefiringline.com/forums "best reloading dies" 11/7/10

70 chuckhawks.com/primers

71 1911forum.com/forums "Educate me on 9mm major" 8/29/12

72 thefiringline.com/forums "Uspsa major/minor" 12/9/08 And "9mm major" 2/27/07

73 forums.brianenos.com "9mm major pressure levels" 3/26/09

74 accurateshooter.com/year–reviews/test–quickload–reviews

75 Multiple sites for static electricity/press grounding
    wikipedia.org/wiki/staticelectricity
    thefiringline.com/forums "Would it make sense to ground my reloading bench/equipment" 1/22/15
    calguns.net/calgunforum
    "How to: basic grounding for your press" 11/6/11
    forums.brianenos.com "running a ground wire to press" 3/1/12

76 reloadersnest.com "Dillon rapid trim" 2/15/10

77 you tube video "Dillon square deal B primer flip solution:"

78 thefiringline.com/forums
    "has anyone used a HIT factor bearing on 650" 8/29/09

79   thetruthaboutguns.com "Gear review: Mr. Bullet Feeder" 3/17/15

80   brownells.com "gun cleaning clinic: Moly coated barrel maintainance" by Steve Schmidt

81   wikipedia.org/wiki/molybdenim disulfide

82   thefirearmsforum.com "truth about moly coated bullets" 7/26/09

83   shootingsoftware.com/moly "the latest on moly"

84   6mmbr.com/normamoly "moly–does it extend barrel life"

     Studies re. barrel life, velocity and pressure. C/O norma precision by Christer Larson R&D

85   SASS Cowboy Chronicle–March 2017 issue, page 56–62.

     "He died from lead poisoning" by Roger Rapid

86   CDC–Agency for toxic substances and disease registry CAS# 7439-92-1

87   Dillon Blue Press, Feb 2017, "Mr. Bullet Feeder and RF-100"

88   The firearmsforum.com, "Questions about resizing rifle brass", Oct. 25,2016. L.D. Bennett

89   you tube, "Fine tuning the Dillon RF-100 to reduce noise, primers flipping and jumping"

90   Dillon Blue Press, June 2017, page 48, article by Duane Thomas.

91   Wikipedia.org/wiki/static electricity.

92   thefiringline.com/forums, "Would it make sense to ground my reloading bench/equipment", 1-22-15.

93   calguns.net/calgunforum, "How to: basic grounding for your press" 11-6-11.

94   forums.brianenos.com/ "Running a ground wire to your press", 3-1-12.

Printed in the United States
By Bookmasters